ΛCCELERΛTE
YOUR IMPACT

ACCELERATE YOUR IMPACT

10 WAYS TO FUEL YOUR NONPROFIT'S FUNDRAISING ENGINE

GENERAL EDITOR
TRENT RICKER

EXECUTIVE EDITOR, **BEN STROUP**

PURSUANT. PUBLISHING

Contents

Introduction

The only thing certain about the future is that it is uncertain. We'd all like to have a proverbial crystal ball and know exactly what is about to happen next. Unfortunately, that doesn't exist. And if it did, our roles might be diminished because the essence of leadership is the ability to move forward in the tension between what we know and what we don't.

One thing we do know is that the climate of fundraising is changing. What has worked in the past is not what will work today—or tomorrow. We must adapt. We must find new ways to apply the fundamentals of fundraising. Only then will we be able to overcome the mounting challenges of our work.

In order to accelerate change, we must become smarter fundraisers. Working smarter means assessing what's working—and what isn't. It means applying both creativity and analytics to ensure we are telling our story to the right people and giving them the chance to respond in measureable and meaningful ways.

This book was created as a practical, actionable guide with you, the nonprofit leader, in mind. My hope is that what you read will inspire and energize you. It takes a strong leader to put aside what's always been done to make room for necessary changes, even if those changes are painful. I trust the information, experience, and encouragement within these pages will better equip you as you lead your organization through the changes.

Despite the relentless challenges you face in acquiring, upgrading, and retaining donors, I believe you have every reason to be hopeful about the future. This is your moment to accelerate your impact on the world!

—Trent Ricker, Pursuant CEO and General Editor

1

Rethinking a Culture of Philanthropy: Key Concepts to Assess an Organization's Culture

GARY M. COLE

It's not uncommon for fundraising practitioners to speak of the *culture of philanthropy* that exists within their organizations. The term itself has become quite popular in recent years. However, what is uncommon is an ability to collectively articulate what exactly the phrase means, how it looks, how it should be measured, and how those whom the organization serves may benefit from such a culture. As catalysts for change, development professionals have perhaps the best vantage point to view the entire organization. But in order to effect change and help create a philanthropic culture, an understanding of organizational culture is first needed.

Organizational Culture

There are two schools of thought on organizational culture. Some believe that organizations *have* cultures. Others believe that organizations *are* cultures. For the purpose of this chapter, organizational culture describes the attitudes, experiences, beliefs, and values of an organization. Simply put, the culture defines how things are done in an organization and how individuals within it interact with one another.

A Culture of Philanthropy

A *culture of philanthropy* refers to an organization's attitude toward philanthropy and the development process. But in this instance, *philanthropy* refers to more than fundraising revenue goals. Practitioners must first understand the value of the organizational culture, the importance of philanthropy, the link between philanthropy and development, and the leadership roles for each of us in this process to truly understand how to create a culture of philanthropy. Even then, there are broader behaviors and practices that must be understood. Following are four key components that will provide a deeper dive into what kind of culture actually exists within your organization. Evidence of a strong culture of philanthropy typically includes:

- demonstrated leadership at all organizational levels
- authentic storytelling and a commitment to conversation with all stakeholders

- mission-driven systems, staffing, structure, and processes
- shared values and a collective commitment to a common goal

Leadership and Followership

Creating a culture of philanthropy within an organization begins at the top. The board's level of engagement is a critical element of a strong philanthropic culture. How often the board meets, the style of the meetings, term limits and rotation schedules, board giving, and the activities of board committees send messages about the value placed upon the board's leadership in philanthropy. Other critical factors are how the board chooses to measure progress toward mission, the impact of philanthropic efforts, and the importance placed on long-term relationships.

But it doesn't end there. What's also required is the ability to lead from the middle—or, quite frankly, wherever your position ranks in the hierarchy. Doing so provides all with the opportunity to impact positive change.

But there are specific aspects to leadership necessary to create a culture of philanthropy beyond the visible willingness of boards to engage in strategy, staff to counsel superiors, or managers to follow subordinates.

Governing boards and senior leadership are responsible for an organization's administration and strategic direction. Where their sustained focus resides says a great deal about the existing culture, climate, and areas of perceived significance.

Philanthropic organizations have missions. They exist to serve society, not to simply provide employment for those working within them. Leadership must maintain a balanced focus on both the organization's impact on society and its operational efficiency. Again, this does not stop at the top, but should penetrate deeply to all levels of the organizations.

Organizational attention drifts far too often. Focus shifts solely on operational efficiencies (the cost of raising a dollar is one example) and tactics, as opposed to measuring the intended impact on those served by the organization and society as a whole. Subsequently, without many noticing, board and internal conversations shift to the organization's needs as opposed to societal needs. Philanthropic support becomes the answer to little more than budgetary gaps, as organizational strategy focuses on maintaining organizational profitability rather than serving others.

This diminishes the case for support and the role of philanthropic investments and those willing to make them, and it marginalizes fundraising practitioners as well. Being an efficient organization does not mean it's more philanthropic.

Being an efficient organization does not mean it's more philanthropic.

The responsibility then rests on the entire organization to maintain focus on the mission. Hanging plaques with the mission statement in offices or asking staff to involuntarily stand and recite the mission at staff meetings does not make an organization more philanthropic. Leading, regardless of your position classification, and following while living the mission creates a more philanthropic culture.

Storytelling

Purposeful and authentic storytelling is vital in any organization, but it is increasingly necessary in philanthropic organizations seeking to engage external support in order to advance the organizational mission. Consensus building, a shared vision, and inclusion in the process are required by both internal and external constituents.

Unfortunately, stories are far too often more monologue than dialogue. Gaining ownership of and commitment to the organization's vision becomes much more difficult when leaders develop a vision for the organization without first soliciting feedback from all key stakeholders. Key stakeholders, who are critical to the success of the vision, are then relegated to the role of spectator rather than being engaged, respected, and active participants.

This practice creates both a disincentive for staff to offer feedback and a diminished desired to engage in the success of the organization with any degree of passion or enthusiasm. As a result, staff simply wait for further instructions before proceeding with any tactical assignment. The result for the organization is a less creative, less autonomous, and less committed staff.

The same concept holds true outside of the walls of the organization. Storytelling must be about meaningful, authentic, two-way conversations when engaging volunteers, advocates, and those willing to make philanthropic investment in the mission. We must spend more time being interested instead of simply trying to be interesting. Our stories must have a goal. They must be memorable, and they must be actionable.

Often organizations create communication plans that lack integration or goals. The plans are measured by the message being delivered as opposed to the message received. Creating a culture of philanthropy requires that all within the organization speak the same language and tell the same story. It requires that all messages and all communication channels become integrated to increase interaction, involve others more meaningfully in the life of the organization, enhance a shared vision, and create viral advocates for the cause. In short, philanthropic organizations are those that move from talking *at* people to talking *with* people—and they do so with purpose and intent.

Creating a culture of philanthropy requires that all within the organization speak the same language and tell the same story.

Systems, Processes, Staffing, and Structure

How we organize ourselves also says a great deal about who we are and what's important to us. There are a number of aspects related to organizational structure that contribute to enhancing an organization's culture of philanthropy. Three aspects of utmost importance are *staffing and structure, systems and processes*, and *reward systems*.

First, examine your current organizational structure. Is it mechanistic and militaristic, or organic and flat? Does it encourage autonomy, decentralized decision making, teamwork, and collaboration?

Second, assess your job descriptions. Do your currently filled positions and their respective job descriptions accurately reflect your intended outcomes? In other words, do the roles delegated to staff reinforce your organizational objectives, or do they undermine them? We often assume the existing staffing and structure promote a culture of philanthropy when they actually promote a culture of charity. There is indeed a difference between the two, but what is it?

A culture of charity is set up to passively receive gifts, whereas a culture of philanthropy is designed to actively pursue philanthropic investments. Functions within a culture of charity tend to focus on fundraising transactions, while a culture of philanthropy focuses on transformational events resulting in philanthropic investments. Additionally, a culture of charity focuses on short-term, fiscal year–based organizational needs. A culture of philanthropy focuses on long-term societal needs and how best to engage others in helping to meet those needs.

It is also important to understand more fully the incentives and reward systems in place for staff when we assess the "things" we do every day when we arrive at work.

Daniel H. Pink, author of the book *Drive: The Surprising Truth about What Motivates Us* (Riverhead, 2011), speaks of three basic motivators: *biological, reward and punishment,* and *interest/purpose/fun.* Biological motivators refer to basic necessities, such as food and water. Reward and punishment (also referred to as "carrot and stick") is most prevalent in organizations today. This activity seeks to reward desired behavior and punish behavior deemed undesirable.

In philanthropic organizations, a director of development may be rewarded by raising more money, or punished if he or she does not. This type of reward system is fear-based and focuses on compliance as opposed to commitment. It focuses on the short-term bottom line instead of long-term growth, and it almost never takes into consideration the many external factors, unique episodic events, or changing variables that may lead to success or inhibit it. Perhaps that's why it is said that a fundraiser is only as good as his or her last campaign (or fiscal year).

A fundraiser is only as good as his or her last campaign (or fiscal year).

The third motivator refers to the things we do because they are fun, and would continue doing even if we were not paid to do them. Ironically, many join nonprofit organizations—and in particular, the fundraising profession—because this form of livelihood is viewed as a vocation. It is an opportunity to serve a cause bigger than the individual, and it allows us to help create a better society and add value and fulfillment to our own lives and the lives of others. But how often are nonprofit professionals and fundraising practitioners allowed the opportunity to go off script, be creative, and offer innovative new solutions? How often are they rewarded for it?

Creating a culture of philanthropy requires that we shift our reward systems so they actually encourage desired behavior while also reinforcing the need for individual ownership, creativity, and commitment to the work being done. The reward systems must be created to reward behavior that is effective for the organization, inspiring for the individual, and most important, proven to advance the organizational mission.

Here are two examples. We often measure success by the number of proposals delivered to individuals or foundations, or the number of magazines and newsletters mailed to constituents in any given fiscal year. In fact, many performance appraisals continue to evaluate activity over outcome.

Unfortunately, this focus and subsequent measurement placed on the action rather than the response correlates little with how efficient and effective an organization is at advancing its mission. Organizations default to measuring the number of solicitations made over the prior year when they should be measuring responses to appeals for support.

We often measure our results by the number of pieces mailed rather than the impact achieved. We should focus less on the circulation of a magazine or newsletter and more on the purpose of our storytelling, the desired response of the reader, and the effectiveness of our call to action.

Shared Values

Shared values, norms, and mutually agreed-upon practices are perhaps the most critical components of a philanthropic learning organization. Shared values are the articulated beliefs that provide the framework to guide actions and judgments within an organization.

These values represent a unique cultural philosophy, not a program. Creating a culture of philanthropy requires determining your organization's specific shared values and how you will reinforce them through practice on a daily basis. Shared values that enhance an organization's collective capacity to excel while also enhancing public trust and confidence in the organization include, but are not limited to, the following:

- **Ethical Behavior:** There's an old joke that says, "Business ethics (in concept) are an oxymoron."

The truth is, there is no room in philanthropic organizations for even the appearance of unethical behavior. Self-dealing and conflicts of interest at the board level should be proactively addressed. Boards should act as exemplary, invested stakeholders and not as entitled shareholders. Unquestioned ethical integrity is paramount as it relates to the treatment of staff and organizational beneficiaries. When working with donors, ethical behavior is required across the continuum of organizational activities. A culture of philanthropy cannot exist if a gift is solicited that is not in the donor's best interest. Organizations must use the gift as agreed upon once it is received. Attention should be given to maintaining ethical practices even in what appears to be the most benign or innocent of settings. For example, donor research should never seek more information than is needed to effectively invite individuals into the organization. Donor confidentiality should be maintained at all costs. Staff should take care to not criticize a donor, even privately among peers, for a gift believed to be less than the donor's perceived capability.

- **Stewardship:** The word *stewardship* has implied a number of things throughout history, but its core meaning has always centered on duty of service and responsibility in management. To imply that a culture of philanthropy exists within an organization suggests that (1) resources are used in the most effective and efficient manner, and the impact of philanthropic dollars, both separately and in contrast with other revenue sources, is well understood throughout the organization and can be demonstrated and articulated; (2) donor intelligence and data analytics are used to inform tactics and strategies; and (3) where possible, every effort is made to segment outreach, prospective donor cultivation, and relevant, constituent-specific reporting on the impact of philanthropic investments.

- **Fail Forward Learning:** Eliminating a culture of fear and punitive retribution for unintended mistakes is a first step in encouraging new ideas and innovation among staff. It should be noted that failure as the result of testing new strategies is not harmful, as long as such failure is neither intentional nor repetitive. Allowing staff to test new techniques, technologies, or strategies should be encouraged and embraced. This sense of empowerment, autonomy, and self-direction helps individuals at all levels experiment, gain ownership in the process, and enjoy the satisfaction when progress is made. When you fail, fail forward. In a philanthropic organization, this concept should apply to volunteers and donors too. Sometimes we have to let board members try new things too.

- **Collaboration and Shared Responsibility:**
  An organization that sequesters philanthropy and
  fundraising to the development office staff severely
  limits its philanthropic potential. To eliminate the
  "not my job" mentality, each individual needs to
  understand the vital role he or she plays in obtaining
  the organization's mission. Collaboration is essential.
  Stories cannot be told if they are not created in the
  first place. A philanthropic organization is one in
  which all within it do what is required to meet its
  objectives. To use a sports analogy, reward assists as
  much as you reward points scored. All employees
  should be champions of the cause to create a culture
  of philanthropy. Opportunities should be sought to
  eliminate redundancy of effort to achieve greater
  efficiency. All should embrace a spirit of service. A
  spirit of collaboration serves as a reminder that
  external constituents can and should play a role
  in advancing the mission. It is this synergy and
  dynamic tension between staff and volunteers that
  can more quickly propel an organization's efforts in
  serving others.

Conclusion

A culture of philanthropy is not a program to be created, but acknowledgment of and adherence to a set of shared values. These shared values guide the manner in which we perceive, believe, evaluate, and act within organizations. The responsibility for creating and maintaining such a culture resides within every individual and every functional program area. Philanthropic organizations by nature are created to serve others. Therefore, those within a philanthropic organization should remain vigilant of the ongoing individual responsibility to the collective process designed to demonstrate those values.

In the next chapter, we will look at how to redefine fundraising "success" so that your stewardship strategy not only *decreases* losses, but also *increases* gains.

2

In the Mind of the Donor: Changing Retention Realities through Strategic Stewardship

ALLISON LEWIS LODHI

Raising more money from fewer donors is a "trend" we've heard so much about in the last decade, it's become accepted as the norm. Allow me to sound the alarm.

What is "normal" is too easily comfortable, and what is comfortable too often becomes expected. Raising more money from fewer donors is not normal; it is an indictment. And it's *not* an indictment of acquisition efforts; rather, the nonprofit sector has been doing an abysmal job of retaining donors. This "trend" is really a reflection of ineffective donor stewardship.

Redefining Fundraising Success

In the *2011 Fundraising Effectiveness Survey Report* by the Association of Fundraising Professionals (AFP) and the

Urban Institute, the data show that for every $5.35 raised, $5.54 was lost through attrition.[1] That's -1.9 percent net growth. In other words, even when annual revenue appears to be positive, after accounting for gifts lost through donor attrition, the overall number is actually negative. That is not sustainable—no matter how commonplace it may be.

How does this happen? Many fundraisers are measured simply on total dollars raised. However, analyzing year-to-year overall *fundraising gains* separately from overall *fundraising losses* in both dollars and donors often paints a very different picture.

It's time to redefine fundraising success. No matter how much money is being raised, donor attrition means missed opportunities to retain and renew. Rather than hop back on the expensive treadmill of finding new donors to fill the holes, it's time for a stewardship strategy that not only decreases losses, but also increases gains.

Stewardship Is about Relationships

We know stewardship is about relationships. When we survey our nonprofit clients, most will initially self-assess their stewardship as being "excellent," yet their data reveal lagging retention, slow second-gift conversion, limited reactivation, and lengthy timelines to get to an upgrade. Research has also consistently concluded that donors overwhelmingly desire

1   http://www.afpnet.org/files/ContentDocuments /FEP2011FinalReport.pdf, p. 8.

more information about how their specific gifts are being used in order for them to feel motivated to keep giving.

A deeper look at nonprofit perspectives reflects a definition of stewardship contingent on the fulfillment of specific activities, such as sending a thank-you, communicating through a newsletter, or delivering the annual report in a timely manner—it can look more like a checklist than a relationship.

From the donor's perspective, stewardship is about taking care of what's been entrusted to us. Yet, if the true definition of *stewardship* is "carefully managing the funds entrusted to us by donors," then how many of our donors would agree that we are "good stewards" when the organization is losing more dollars and donors than it gains each year?

We must connect our stewardship practices to *our responsibility to care for what's been entrusted to us*, and then take the next step to *reassure the donors* of that care. By shifting our perspective away from the stewardship checklist and toward the connection that a donor feels with our organization, we have more opportunities to engage the donor and enhance the relationship.

Remembering What It's Like to Be the Donor

After years of working in fundraising, it's easy to lose track of what it *feels like* to be the donor—to send a gift and then wonder what it was used for or why you haven't heard back. Or to feel astonished that your small, onetime generosity would trigger monthly solicitations before any type of acknowledgment is received. We forget what it feels like to just be "added to the file," rather than being treated the way we feel—*as a human being investing in an important cause*. As fundraisers, we would be wise to think of stewardship from the donor's perspective.

What Makes Effective Donor Stewardship

Recently, I had the honor and privilege of interviewing donors about stewardship. These donors offered many salient reminders of why people give and the kind of inspiration they need to continue doing so. While this information represents a small cross section of donors and not a broad-based scientific study, what they communicated validates everything the big studies have already told us.

Here's what the donors said:

> "Your receipt tells me you got my gift. Your thank-you letter tells me why it mattered."

Why do the receipt and thank-you letter HAVE to go out within forty-eight hours of receiving the gift? It's not because "it's procedure" but because *our timeliness gives donors confidence* that the gift was received. It communicates a positive first impression that the gift will be put to use effectively.

A donation is not a shopping experience. On the contrary, people give because they have an emotional connection with the organization. Your response to that first gift sets the stage for what's going to happen next in the relationship.

This first interaction should instill confidence that making the gift was a good decision. It should immediately tell the story of how the gift will be put to good use. Then tell the donor how and when he or she will hear more—an e-mail in three weeks?

When you instill confidence over and over again through every interaction, that feeling becomes a lifelong part of the donor's experience with the organization.

A newsletter next quarter? Remember, donors don't know our processes. When you instill confidence over and over again through every interaction, that feeling becomes a lifelong part of the donor's experience with the organization.

> "My gift is personal, and I'd like my thank-you letter to come from someone who knows me or the purpose of my gift. Yes, the personalized letter and signature are worth the effort."

Nonprofits often establish business rules and processes to generate thank-you receipts at the proper time or to distribute a quarterly newsletter as one piece of the stewardship pie. We automate these functions to avoid anything falling through the cracks or to save staff time for the "more important" efforts. We perpetuate such practices because we think we're supposed to. Often these processes have no connection to the manner in which the gift was given. Even worse, the messaging misses the opportunity to point donors to the next step in their relationship with the organization. Consider what really moves the needle in a donor relationship, and then focus your energy there, eliminating other activities.

> "Whether good or bad, I want to hear news about the organization directly *from* the organization, not from the news channel or my neighbors."

If we truly want to have a relationship with our donors, we should plan to communicate with them in an appropriate manner—they should be the "first to know" in good times and in bad. It's a sign of respect toward those who care enough to give.

Donors should be the "first to know" in good times and in bad. It's a sign of respect toward those who care enough to give.

And in those times of good and bad, timeliness of response is really a function of readiness. Do we have proactive plans and possibly prewritten press releases for how we'll respond in a crisis? Do we have succession plans and a communication strategy to stay ahead of turnover, especially with key leadership? Do we celebrate success with our donors?

Our core communications job, as a function of stewardship, is to maintain credibility and trustworthiness.

> "Your name in my in-box or mailbox is a good reminder that we have a relationship. I don't read everything you send, but you are there, where others aren't."

Consider that sometimes the value of a communication piece is simply the touch point. Donors are asking us to match content, format, and length to the communication's purpose—we need to know what we want donors to do, feel, or think. Why do we send donors a wordy quarterly newsletter? None of them are begging for 2,500 words to read in their spare time. Instead, one brief story can reassure the donor about how new gifts are making a difference. Not everything we send to donors needs to be overly produced. Of course, the key is knowing when it matters and when it doesn't.

Time-sensitive news should be short, sweet, and easy to consume. A human-interest piece should be thoughtful, planned out, and published in a format suitable to its length. And the effort put into those longer pieces can be leveraged in other formats, edited down so it can be incorporated into a thank-you letter, newsletter article, or social media post.

Hearing the same snippet in variations is just fine.

It's time we take a look at every step of the stewardship process and examine the reasons behind the content, timing, and distribution of each message.

> "If you make a mistake, I'll understand if you tell me personally, promptly, and in a straightforward manner, with thoughts on how to prevent it from happening again."

Surprise, surprise! Donors know we are human . . . and they're okay with it. So often, we operate in extremes, assuming that donors will leave us if we make a mistake. Of course we have to be competent professionals. But how we *handle* a mistake often says more about the nonprofit and its commitment to its donors than the mistake itself.

> "If you ask me for another gift that isn't my interest, find out what [my interest] is and come back. You may have misunderstood my passion, but it's not over!"

Know thy donor. And if you don't know, ask. Part of stewarding an existing donor relationship is demonstrating that you understand the donor's giving motivations and values. Donors say that occasionally fundraisers will miss the mark, and then, strangely, they just go away. Perhaps this is done out of embarrassment or a lack of knowing what to do next; but whatever the reason might be, they stop asking or visiting their donors.

Know thy donor. And if you don't know, ask . . . Donors are happy to tell you all about their passions.

Donors are happy to tell you all about their passions. They'll do so not only when asked, but also through their behaviors. Know what content your donors are interacting with, reading, and forwarding. Have a strategy to collect this information and tailor future content or solicitations accordingly.

Donors will feel more personally connected when they hear about what interests them, and you will maximize the likelihood that they'll stick around. The key is to see it through until you understand the donors' motivations and passions. And as one donor said, "No, really. Come back. So many never ask again. How could I say no to a gift I designed?"

"Let me experience my philanthropy either
in person or digitally if I can't be there."

Your donors can't be everywhere you are. But if you're there, you can easily bring them along through webcam, video, or photography. Show them what you're doing to save the rain forest or how you're increasing access to medical care for children in that rural village. People want to be a part of something. Create an experience so they can witness their gifts in action no matter how far away they live.

A key part of the stewardship strategy is planning intentional next steps in the donor relationship. It should be an unfolding story that feels natural. It's about predetermining what happens at each step of the process for every type of gift. No matter the initial connection point—a mailing, an event, face-to-face contact, or otherwise—you should already know how donors will experience the first ask, what your thank-you message will say, and how it will point them to the next series of communications. You know in advance the next piece of the story that you want them to receive. THEN you integrate these next steps into your business rules so it's clear how you'll move donors exactly where you want them to go following their initial and subsequent interactions.

> "Immerse me in the lives of the people my
> gift touches."

Oh, how easily we become impressed with ourselves—*our* facilities, *our* programs, *our* rankings. Donors want to understand how their gifts impact *people*. An endowed chair in the anthropology department might inspire lots of newsletter stories and event invitations about anthropology, which may be of interest. But this does not, on its own, deepen the donor relationship. The donor wants to know how that endowed chair helped recruit a top faculty member, what that professor has written, what students say about his or her teaching, and how students and graduates have been inspired in their learning or careers. It's a subtle but important difference to talk about the people affected rather than where the gift is held in account.

Even smaller gifts can be stewarded in this way. Tell donors how their gifts were pooled to support a larger priority and how lives were changed for the better.

Secrets We Keep from Our Donors

Another flaw in the traditional stewardship model is the practice of determining our stewardship strategy by gift amount, treating donors like a number. It is shortsighted to expect donors to be motivated by what we haven't yet revealed to them. But that's exactly what we're doing when we steward a $10,000 donor differently than a $100 donor. Lower-level donors have no idea what's waiting at the higher stewardship level, so what's enticing them to give more?

Instead of assuming that a smaller gift indicates a decreased likelihood to give more (which is a defeatist perspective), we should strategically over-steward those lower-level donors in an effort to move them to a higher level. Stewardship should be based on the donor's potential, not on a dollar amount. Wouldn't a highly connected authority figure who regularly introduces new prospects to your organization merit a great stewardship strategy, regardless of his or her giving level?

Key Performance Indicators for Measuring Effectiveness

Do these donors' sentiments sound familiar? Do you want to gain a better perspective on your stewardship effectiveness? These four key performance indicators can help you evaluate opportunities to improve your stewardship.

> ***Donor life cycle migration*** is the progression a donor makes in moving from being a prospect to the first and second gift, to upgrading the amount, to multiyear gifts, and finally to major giving. What would change about your strategy if you knew the average time it takes to move someone from prospect to donor or from first gift to second gift? What if you knew the percentage of donors who gave a second gift in that average time frame? Or how quickly (or slowly!) a donor moves from an annual gift to a major gift? This could inform your decisions about stewarding donors at each step in the process, and help you build a strategy to expedite the timeline dramatically.

> ***Cross-channel donor movement*** functions just like any other human relationship. Deeper personal relationships

aren't limited to just one method of communication. You communicate with your spouse in person, on the phone, by text or e-mail, or over a meal. When donors interact with your organization across several different channels (e-mail, web, social media, telemarketing, events, face-to-face, direct mail, etc.), it's indicative of deeper engagement. The deeper the relationship, the higher the lifetime value to your organization.

Real retention metrics identify the individual donor who has stuck with the organization over time. Aggregate retention measures can be misleading. For example, an organization with 3,000 donors last year and 3,100 donors this year appears to have great retention. But we must look at the gains and losses separately. If the organization lost 1,500 donors this year but gained 1,600 first-time donors, then the acquisition numbers look great, but there's clearly a retention problem. Even the best acquisition program can't make up for something that's amiss later on in the donor life cycle and causing donors not to renew. Conversion to a second gift and the factors leading to multiyear loyalty must also be closely examined.

The critical ratios, such as the cost of acquiring and retaining donors over the life cycle, are important to measure. Don't just consider the current year's data. Look at several years at a time, and measure dollars as well as donors. One year of data for an acquisition campaign will seem overly costly at first glance. But a decision to throw out a campaign for that reason alone might as well be a decision to toss out the acquired donors as well. Your willingness to look at ratios over the long term will provide the information you need to determine stewardship effectiveness.

What? No Stewardship Budget?

Since retaining existing donors costs significantly less money than attracting new ones, stewardship should be one of your highest priorities. Think you have no budget? What is stewardship if not marketing? Piggyback onto what your organization's marketing department is doing and invest some of those dollars into donor retention. Be intentional about making the donor's first stewardship interaction just as fabulous as the marketing that got them in the door in the first place.

The savvy fundraiser invests in stewardship activities that target donors with the highest potential to become better donors. Examine your donors' relationships to your organization, along with their level of interest and ability to give, and you'll find those people who are the most connected and, therefore, worth the extra stewardship effort.

Integrated Stewardship

Developing a strategy for integrated stewardship ultimately contributes to better donor retention. The following five components are key to building a fluid relationship with the donor from the first interaction:

STRATEGY: Thoughtful and planned communications with an emotional connection

CONSISTENCY: Reflects a common inspirational message throughout

INTEGRATION: Anticipates cross-channel interactions

CONGRUENCE: Leverages channel strengths by providing just the right amount of content

INTENTIONALITY: Drives donors toward stated goals

Examine every aspect of your stewardship strategy. Is each piece part of an overall integrated approach? Or do the pieces stand alone and with little connection to the emotional story your donors experience as they get to know your organization?

Invest in the Relationship

Stewardship is more than just a box to check; it's the most substantial portion of your fundraising strategy. When nonprofit dollars are spent to capture first-time donors who are subsequently lost after their first gift, it's not just a budgetary issue. It's a loss of funds that might have been invested in programs instead. That, in itself, is poor stewardship.

If you've been alarmed by this "trend" of fewer donors, it's time to pause, evaluate your data, and examine your stewardship priorities—what they are and what they should be, as well as how they fit into the complete picture of your development plan. Then take the next steps to modify your stewardship practices to ensure that you're building true relationships with your donors. It's one of the most cost-conscious ways to improve fundraising effectiveness.

Pursuant has clients whose donor retention rates have exceeded 70 percent after putting these strategies into practice! While your "results may vary," there is no question that strong stewardship practices will reverse the trends reported by the Association of Fundraising Professionals.

Let us know when you're ready. We can help.

In the next chapter we will look at new ways of thinking about your capital campaign. Sometimes the old ways work, sure, but when they don't, what do you do? That's what you'll learn next.

3

The New Comprehensive Capital Campaign

GARY M. COLE

While preparing to write the white paper from which this chapter was developed, I Googled the phrase "this isn't your father's . . ." to see what would surface. I expected the tagline ending ". . . Oldsmobile." I did not expect to see more than 60 million hits, including these:

> This isn't your father's . . .
>> . . . Jim Beam
>> . . . Panzer Dragoon
>> . . . Halo Combat
>> . . . New York Federal Reserve
>> . . . recession
>> . . . dormitory

Indeed, times have changed, including the environment in which we raise funds and conduct capital campaigns. Changes in technology, communication tools, expectations, and even the pace of life all demand that we take a fresh look at the tactics and methodologies we use to engage donors.

This is what led Pursuant to embrace an organizational commitment to *redefining fundraising* with both the confidence and humility that come from serving the philanthropic vision of tens of thousands of life-changing organizations. Adopted as a corporate tagline, the statement signifies both a collective commitment to helping organizations challenge long-held assumptions and identify new "best practices," while also acknowledging our century-long legacy of innovation in the nonprofit sector. In fact, redefining fundraising is the very legacy started in the early twentieth century by the initial visionaries preserved in the Ketchum name. Pursuant is simply acknowledging and recommitting to a vision of innovation and optimization that was truly radical in its day and changed the face of organized philanthropy forever.

No, this isn't your father's capital campaign. But before we dive into some of the changes in organized philanthropy now being instituted in the twenty-first century, let's take a quick look back at what changed a hundred years ago when Carlton and George Ketchum participated in an extraordinary campaign for the University of Pittsburgh.

A Legacy of Innovation and Optimization

In January 1914, Charles Sumner Ward, who was gaining a national reputation for his success in deploying intensive and short-term fundraising initiatives for the YMCA, was summoned by Chancellor Samuel McCormick of the University of Pittsburgh to assist in raising $3 million to develop its new campus in Pittsburgh. Though he had never conducted a campaign for an educational institution, Ward devised a strategy for a ten-day campaign, similar to those he'd conducted for the YMCA. The chancellor appointed two assistants, brothers Carlton and George Ketchum, to assist Ward in directing this ambitious effort. And at its conclusion, $2.1 million was raised.

One hundred years later, the sums raised during that ten-day initiative remain impressive. However, there was a greater lesson for the newly emerging field of organized philanthropy. The Ketchum brothers recognized that a best practice for one organization may not be applicable or transferable to other organizations within the nonprofit sector. Ward's YMCA model and Ketchum's refinement and optimization for use in large-scale national efforts resulted in a capital campaign model embraced by both fundraising counsel and nonprofit organizations throughout the last century.

Looking back at our nation's first campaigns, Carlton Ketchum noted:

One of the characteristics of the early college capital fund campaigns was that their planning customarily ignored annual alumni funds if such existed. Campaigners and colleges learned the hard way that this did not pay . . . The early college fund campaigns, being patterned on those for the YMCA and like institutions, were short-term. Since most of them were chiefly local, appealing to the college's community, this was possible, but as they broadened out, it took a few years' experience to demonstrate that a lot more time needed to be allowed for them.

Time-Tested Elements of Campaigns

The essential elements of a campaign in the early 1900s featured words such as: *concentration, organization, sacrifice, education, cumulative effect,* and *civic impulse.* A campaign plan would seek to ensure that

- the organization was in suitable condition to go before the public with a plea for support
- the board of directors weighed the plan carefully, understood the sacrifice involved, and committed unreservedly to it

- an approximate date for the campaign was set months ahead so that detailed preparations could take place before launch
- in an advance publicity campaign through the press, the public would be kept informed of the need for which funds were being raised (typically a building)
- one large subscription equaling 10 to 30 percent of the goal would be secured contingent upon raising the entire amount in the allotted time (ten days to one month)
- all directors would be prepared to make their subscription (gift) as soon as the campaign launched to serve as an example to others
- a list of prospective subscribers would be prepared and placed on cards
- assignments would be distributed to volunteer solicitors

Over the last ten decades, these campaign elements, refined by Ketchum and the legacy team of what has today become Pursuant Ketchum, were adopted and used as guides to ensure success by fundraising counsel, organizational staff, and volunteers alike. And as technology has advanced, the number of nonprofit organizations has grown, and the competition for charitable dollars has increased exponentially, the need for Pursuant's leadership in designing, implementing, and evaluating fundraising strategies has never been greater.

The Modern Pursuant Ketchum Campaign

Though many of the campaign essentials previously mentioned have become hallmarks of Pursuant's approach to capital campaign design and implementation, failure to acknowledge the new realities of fundraising in the twenty-first century will most certainly impede efforts and prevent success. Building upon these proven principles vetted through ten decades of successful campaign execution, Pursuant has evolved the most comprehensive and robust approach available to nonprofits today, responding to essential shifts in donor behavior, available technology, and the market realities of the twenty-first century.

Begin with the Five Campaign Essentials

Pursuant's extensive experience in campaigns has helped us identify five campaign essentials that we include in every evaluation of campaign readiness. These essentials have been found to be critical to the success of a campaign:

- **Leadership:** The success of any capital campaign is dependent upon strong volunteer leadership. We recognize the role of leadership involves strategic planning, cultivating engaged and committed followers, and driving action. Thus, we evaluate the presence of influential and respected leaders as active champions in the campaign.

- **Case for Support:** The case for support must be an emotionally compelling and persuasive demonstration that the campaign is absolutely necessary, one which highlights the unique qualities of the organization. Constituents take a fundraising effort seriously when they're convinced the need is valid, urgent, and compelling.

- **Sufficient Contributable Dollars:** Pursuant assesses the number of prospects needed to raise the required funds, and confirms that the proper proportion of prospects relative to fundraising capacity is available. Interviews with prospective donors are conducted to ensure that campaign goals are targeted to donor interests and are realistic.

- **Adequate Resources:** Verifying adequate internal resources is a prerequisite for conducting a successful campaign. Allocating sufficient resources to a key strategic initiative such as a campaign is vital to success. Resources include staff and skills, structure, systems and processes, and even volunteer support.

- **Well-Organized Campaign Cabinet:** Beyond recruiting strong volunteer leadership, the manner in which leadership members are identified, enlisted, expanded, and managed is vital to success. Pursuant gives significant attention to creating a well-organized and well-managed campaign cabinet that will lead by example.

New Realities of Capital Campaigns

In addition to our time-tested campaign essentials, Pursuant has recognized new realities confronting institutions, their leaders, and those who support them, including these:

- **It is essential to create personal conversations with donors through communication to the masses.** Campaigns have grown in size and sophistication over the last century. Ten-day efforts to raise hundreds of thousands to several million dollars have evolved into five-, seven-, and ten-year efforts designed to raise hundreds of millions to billions of dollars. As a result, the number of donors required to meet such efforts has grown exponentially as well. Communicating campaign case elements through the media prior to a kickoff has become outdated and ineffective. Growth in the nonprofit sector and competition for charitable dollars requires personalized one-to-one multichannel communication to thousands. Moreover, developing "behavioral interest profiles" based on how donors interact with you helps an organization develop the right ask for the right donor at the right time.

- **Organizations need to utilize and leverage all communication channels in an integrated strategy.** Early campaigns primarily utilized face-to-face solicitations and special events to achieve success. As campaigns have grown over the last fifty years, so have technological advancements and opportunities to communicate with donors. Despite these advancements, organizations are realizing that little thought has been given to how best to leverage all communication channels for donor cultivation, solicitation, and recognition; how to test the effectiveness of each channel; and how to measure return on investment to ensure good stewardship of organizational resources.

- **Deepening relationships with existing donors is vital during each campaign.** Modern campaigns have become more than once-in-a-lifetime opportunities for charitable support. They represent episodic events in the life of an organization, requiring continued philanthropic investments over time, versus simple, one time charitable contributions. They require emphasis on the transformational relationship between a donor and a cause, as opposed to the transactional exchange between a supporter and a charity. Significant philanthropic investments require deepened engagements and relationships with donors. As today's campaigns grow in size and scope, ignoring this reality can be detrimental to success.

- **Identifying and acquiring new donors and future leaders is a must for continued campaign**

success. Ongoing needs necessitate a plan for identifying ongoing leadership and support. As capital campaigns grow in size and scope, so too does the need for future supporters and organizational leadership. Ignoring donor acquisition and leadership development as significant components of any campaign strategy suggests an unbalanced focus on institutional needs versus societal impact. Today, feasibility studies should include an assessment of both the availability and the interest of those capable of making pace-setting leadership gifts, and the availability of mid-level donors. Such a comprehensive approach requires more than the qualitative assessments of the past; quantitative empirical review of the entire donor base becomes critical. In an atmosphere where preparation for the next campaign often begins shortly after the last campaign's completion, every campaign becomes an opportunity to cultivate mid-level donors who could be the next campaign's leaders.

- **Organizations must prioritize and segment donors for effective cultivation and solicitation based on data.** Those with the greatest philanthropic capacity, relationship with the organization, and inclination to support the needs identified in the case for support will typically receive the highest cultivation and solicitation priority at the launch of any campaign. But as campaign goals increase and needs move from modular projects (such as building a new facility) to comprehensive efforts, understanding how to prioritize and segment donors based on organizational objectives and donor interest in a donor-focused, mission-driven approach becomes even more critical. Understanding how to accomplish such a feat when the need is for the prospect pool to grow from the top one hundred donors to thousands demands the ability to prioritize and segment for effective use of staff and volunteer time. This means that traditional manual prospect research inevitably falls short. Using advanced data analytics and predictive modeling allows reliable ranking and penetration of the donor base at every level, ensuring efficiency in outreach and exponentially improving the efficacy of traditional capacity and RFM (recency, frequency, and monetary) scoring.

- **Organizations should always be positioning themselves for the next campaign.** Early campaigns in the United States, from the turn of the century

Organizations should always be positioning themselves for the next campaign.

to the last few decades, were positioned as periodic activities separate and apart from ongoing resource-building efforts. As such, these events typically had distinct preplanning, launch, and celebration periods. Such strategies resulted in organizations ramping up communication efforts before a campaign in order to best prepare donors for the ask when the campaign was launched. Inadvertently, this caused organizations to focus on the event (the ask) rather than the relationship with the donor. Contemporary thinking and reflection on these practices have enlightened us to the shortsightedness and inward focus of such behavior. Organizations failing to adopt donor-centric strategies and look beyond the current short-term needs will be less successful in deepening long-term relationships with donors.

So now you know the new realities that you will face as you go about the business of acquiring, cultivating, and soliciting donors. Now it's time to look at a specific type of donor—the *mid-level donor*—and what you need to know about this important constituent.

4

Seven Things You Need to Know about Mid-Level Donors

TONY SMERCINA

Thirteen years of research and practice have uncovered critical insights about mid-level donors: Who are they? How should we communicate with them? How do we secure a gift? We're about to share with you our discoveries on mid-level donors, their importance in future major gifts, and the revolutionary approach that is proven to produce unprecedented results.

The Donor Sombrero

The *donor pyramid* is all too familiar to fundraising professionals— it is the simple framework that represents successful donor cultivation, and our ultimate goal of upgrading and retaining donors into higher levels of giving. Top donors give major gifts, the general masses contribute annual support, and between those two is an area we call *mid-level giving*.

In 2011, former president Bill Clinton spoke at an AFP conference in Chicago, sharing his challenges in fundraising for the Clinton Library. He noted that the majority of contributions were donations from the bottom of the pyramid, or large gifts of $500,000 or more from those at the top. But there weren't many donations in between. This isn't unheard-of in fundraising, but do you really think that it's because people only want to give at the bottom or the top?

A lack of focus on cultivating the donor group between the wide base of annual fund contributors and the smaller core of major-gift donors, resulting in a collapsed donor pyramid.

The reality is that too many organizations focus only on the top and bottom of the donor pyramid, lacking an intentional focus on developing the middle. When this happens, the pyramid loses shape—and thus, its purpose—and becomes what we call the "donor sombrero."

Why is it that so many organizations lack a focused mid-level giving strategy? Here are a few common reasons:

- "There's too much opportunity at the top of the pyramid. It isn't cost-effective for major gift officers to give personal attention to mid-level prospects."
- "We already receive a few mid-tier gifts through other channels, like mail and phone. We just don't have the manpower to tackle the mid-tier."
- "We want to improve mid-level giving, but we just don't know where to start."

> *Too many organizations focus only on the top and bottom of the donor pyramid, lacking an intentional focus on developing the middle. When this happens, the pyramid loses shape—and thus, its purpose.*

The Big Secret

Mid-level giving isn't just a source of giving for today; it is a cultivation strategy for the major donors of tomorrow. There is a cost-effective way to secure mid-level commitments today and develop the pipeline for future major donors: well-trained development officers making personalized, face-to-face visits with prospects who have a high likelihood of giving, and securing mid-level, multiyear giving commitments. Most organizations have a rich source of untapped opportunity in the middle of the pyramid that they overlook. The middle of your pyramid holds valuable opportunity, but getting results requires an informed strategy and specific knowledge about your mid-level prospect pool.

Here are seven things you need to know about your mid-level donors:

1. They look like low-level donors. Many organizations focus major giving efforts on donors who are above the $50,000 mark. And for those who fall below that threshold, nonprofits tend to apply a general annual fund communications strategy. If you could identify the low-level donors and non-donors in your file who have the propensity and capability to contribute at a higher level, would you continue to lump them into your annual fund communications strategy? Identifying these prospects is the first step in a cost-effective mid-level giving strategy. Which prospects display a high affinity and interest toward your organization? Who is most capable of making these gifts? What kind of information do you collect about your constituents?

DONOR PROFILING

Identifying and prioritizing prospects with a higher likelihood of giving based on affinity (behavioral data), capacity (wealth data), and past giving behavior (RFM)

Some of our clients that have been most successful with this program have been Greek organizations. This is because Greek fraternities and foundations are member-based, and therefore tend to be very diligent and disciplined in keeping records. They also engage with their members on a consistent basis. Nonprofits of all shapes and sizes can learn a valuable lesson from Greek organizations—intentionally engaging your constituency generates wealthy piles of behavioral interest data with every point of communication. When that data is collected and analyzed properly, it can be used to inform the prospecting process. Prioritizing prospects based on affinity (behavioral data), capacity (wealth data), and past giving behavior (RFM) is what we call *donor profiling*.

Bottom line: The intelligence we get from donor profiling is invaluable because it allows us to identify prospects with a higher likelihood of giving.

2. They may have never donated to your organization before—on any level. One of the statistics that continues to drop jaws is the rate of new donor acquisition that we have seen: a whopping 70 percent of mid-level gifts secured through the face-to-face strategy were from non-donors. Why would so many individuals who had never made a gift now be inclined to make a significant mid-level commitment? The reasons can differ depending on organization and donor, but the vast majority of new mid-level donors were identified through donor profiling to have a high level of affinity and the financial capacity to give.

Bottom line: Don't overlook your non-donors. They may be your biggest prospect pool.

3. They will give on the first ask. Even for new donors, we have seen a very high rate of securing gifts on the very first ask. In fact, out of the 17,000 prospects we have identified and visited, 41 percent of them have signed a multiyear giving commitment. Consider that statistic—a 41 percent close rate in asking for any size gift is simply astounding. What we have learned is that mid-level gifts do not require a dozen "moves" and several years of cultivation. To secure a gift on the first ask, you need to ensure that you have intelligently identified the top prospects, and that you have a trained development officer who can conduct the right conversation that leads to a gift.

Bottom line: Securing commitments on the first ask requires the right conversation with the right prospect.

4. They need to hear a different message than low-level donors and major donors hear. When you continue to treat low-level donors only as lower-tier prospects, you're overlooking a pool of donors who will respond to personal attention—a pool of donors who may not be aware of their own impact. Organizations must take an active stance to drive low-level donors to the middle of the pyramid—and engage them with the right message. Mid-level prospects won't come knocking on your door on their own because they haven't been shown that they are of great importance to the organization. You can choose to continue communicating with them as you would your lower-tier prospects—with minor nods to personalization—but you're losing your chance to fill the mid-level giving gap and your future major gifts pipeline.

> *"I'm impressed by this new program of talking with mid-level contributors. I never pictured myself as somebody who warranted the personal attention, but it sure made a difference today. I sincerely wish you and the rest of the Association success with meeting your goals."*
> —*Anonymous donor, Association of Former Students, Texas A&M University*

Organizations must take an active stance to drive low-level donors to the middle of the pyramid—and engage them with the right message.

It seems as though it would be easy to deploy major gift officers to make mid-level visits, but it's important to know that the mid-level giving conversation needs to be targeted to mid-level prospects, and that is much different from the conversations major gift officers should have with their prospects. Plus, major gift officers are expensive, and there's simply too much opportunity at the top of the pyramid to make it a cost-effective effort.

Woody Allen once said that 80 percent of success is in showing up, but you need more than that when fundraising for the middle of the pyramid. Face-to-face engagement is key, but what you say is just as critical as actually being there.

In our early years, we learned how important it is to hire the right people to make mid-level visits. A development officer can be great at getting face-to-face meetings with prospects, but if he or she can't conduct the right conversation that leads to a gift, you've lost another valuable opportunity. It is vital that the conversation drives and opens the door for the donor to be responsive. It takes intensive training and ongoing support for officers to successfully engage a prospect, especially a non-donor, and compel that person to make a gift.

Bottom line: Interaction via print and e-mail won't win donors over; they need face-to-face attention to show them their value. Mid-level gift officers must be able to convey the case in a compelling, action-oriented manner to get meaningful results.

5. They will give a significant gift if you have the right system in place. The development officers we deploy for our clients are trained to secure multiyear commitments that are paid via credit card on a monthly basis. Monthly giving is a valuable behavior that shows ongoing commitment to your organization. Furthermore, it is an effective way to lift donors and encourage them to upgrade their contributions. Consider this: An organization decides to offer a premium only to donors who will write a check for $500 or more. What if they were to give away the premium to anyone willing to make a monthly commitment of $75 or more over the next three years?

You think you can't ask a young donor for a significant gift? Think again. Our average gift commitment across the board exceeds $2,000—and that's just the initial engagement. If you have a system in place to process automatic monthly credit card transactions, monthly giving commitments can be extremely valuable for your mid-level program.

Bottom line: Asking for multiyear commitments fulfilled in monthly payments is an effective way to upgrade low-level donors because it makes contributing a mid-level gift an easier and more comfortable financial decision.

6. They are typically supporting between three and seven other organizations. With so many other organizations competing for your donor's dollar, it is increasingly important to engage and connect your constituency beyond typical donor communications. To engage donors in mid-level giving, you need to be one of their top three charitable priorities. You need to move even further up their list if you hope to build your major giving pipeline. So how do you do that? Build a personal relationship. Show them that you're willing to meet with them in person. Do you think they're being visited by their alma mater, or any other organization, when they're not a major donor?

Bottom line: Direct, personalized attention in a cost-efficient manner will help propel your organization into your donors' top three organizations—which is where you need to be.

7. They represent a base of future major donors. Mid-level giving is a cultivation strategy that can lead to major gifts. It is important that you view your mid-level donors as future major donors, because the relationship you establish today can serve to position your prospects to be major donors down the road. You can't expect donors to lift their giving from $100 to $100,000 without the intentional cultivation that larger gifts require. Donors with high financial capacity (and major giving potential) may view a mid-level gift as a comfortable entry point—and are much more likely to take that step if they are cultivated within a personal relationship.

Nonprofit organizations often fall into the bad habit of treating donors as numbers, especially in the context of a churn kind of program. Even if you do receive some mid-level gifts with a churn-driven strategy, you can cross those donors off your future major donors list.

Moving donors upward from the middle of the pyramid requires intentional cultivation and personal relationship building that typical churn programs lack. With every point of contact, you have to keep this in mind: it's all about the relationship.

Bottom line: Be sincere about developing a relationship from the starting point through mid-level gifts and you will cultivate a future base of major donors.

Conclusion

A mid-level giving strategy will add shape and function back to your donor pyramid, helping you lift low-level donors as well as build your pipeline of major donors. Doing this cost-effectively

Moving donors upward from the middle of the pyramid requires intentional cultivation and personal relationship building that typical churn programs lack. With every point of contact, you have to keep this in mind: it's all about the relationship.

requires intelligent identification of prospects, trained mid-level development officers who can close, and a compelling case for support. Easier said than done, right? For organizations that have the donor sombrero problem, it can be difficult to uncover their rich, untapped opportunity because they are typically not equipped with the expertise and/or staff to implement this strategy. In fact, that's the very reason why our clients partner with us. The good news is that if you're one of these donor sombrero organizations, you can start making progress now by educating yourself on mid-level donors. In thirteen years of practice, our organizations that have had the most dramatic success with this program have had three things in common:

1. They wanted a cost-effective way to bridge the top and bottom of the pyramid.
2. They made an organization-wide commitment to mid-level giving as a focused part of their program.
3. They adhered to the principles of the strategy.

Bill Clinton's keynote remark about the donor pyramid is on point, but for those of us in philanthropy who have struggled to retain and upgrade donors and fill the major giving pipeline, it isn't a groundbreaking revelation. The groundbreaking revelation is that the middle of the pyramid is empty not because of donor behavior, but because we keep it empty. There are mid-level donors we are burying in the bottom of the pyramid with our annual fund letters and mass solicitations, but they don't belong there. They belong in the middle of the pyramid—and someday, the top.

In the next chapter, we will talk about "big data"—and how you can use it to your advantage.

5

Turning Big Data into Donations

CURT SWINDOLL

No subject on the *Harvard Business Review* blog has gotten more airtime recently than the subject of "big data." It was a fairly foreign term just a few years ago, but now commercial firms everywhere (and even some nonprofits) are wondering how they can translate customer data into sales. For donation-driven nonprofits, the question is the same: How can we turn donor data into donor intelligence and, ultimately, donor donations?

After reading many articles about this topic, it seems to me that these authors assume that the trip to bountiful is paved and obvious. But that isn't reality. I continue to observe some foundational needs for working through the process of turning donor data into fundraising strategies, and ultimately, into donor support. So that is the purpose of this chapter. As a company committed to data-driven strategies, Pursuant is constantly converting data into decisions on behalf of our clients.

Here is how we do it.

Data Cleanliness

The process of driving strategies from data must begin with an understanding of the data at hand. What does it represent? Is it specific to a certain channel (online only, events only)? Does it cover only some donors (major donors, cash gifts)? Because many donor management systems do a lousy job of capturing all donor data, it's highly likely that you deal with multiple "data stores" or databases of donor information. And that's fine. But it also means your conclusions will be specific to the data you've analyzed.

Another question concerns the time period of the data. Does it cover entire prior years and only part of the current year? Is it up-to-date? Make sure your analysis compares like periods. Analyzing a partial current year is fine as long as it's being compared to the same period of time in the prior year.

Yet another question concerns "outliers" or unusual circumstances. If the data includes a single gift of $1 million and your organization doesn't normally take receipt of gifts that large, then it may be important for you to filter highly unusual gifts out of your analysis. While including such a gift may be appropriate for evaluating the effectiveness of your major donor reps, it's inappropriate for calculating the average gift size across all donations.

Finally, it's critical that you consider the source. How clean is your data? What are the "business rules" governing the use and meaning of codes? How about the data entry process? Have fields been used to store data that are not indicative of the labels attached to those fields? Enterprising nonprofits will store data just about anywhere to make sure there is a record of it—even if it means using fields for data that were never meant to be used that way!

Our database staff at Pursuant will tell you that the process of receiving, cleaning, and understanding client data is some of the most challenging work we do. And they may be right. It's important to verify that the data you think you're evaluating is indeed the data that you're evaluating.

Data Preparation

Just as pictures are worth a thousand words, graphs can represent—and misrepresent—a thousand numbers. So why do we use them? Very simply—we do it to show relationships. The number "$10,000,000" is meaningless unless I tell you that it represents someone's compensation for a year, or it was the gross domestic product (GDP) of an entire country. Context and relationships are everything in analytics.

Graphs are also valuable for digesting vast amounts of data very quickly. Give me a table with one hundred rows, and it may take me several minutes to find the largest and smallest numbers, to see the general trend across all of the numbers, and to evaluate the sizes of the numbers relative to each other. But if we turn that table into a bar chart, then the data relationships come to life.

Conversely, when poor graphing techniques or the wrong graphing form are used, the pictures quickly become misleading. Consider the following charts:

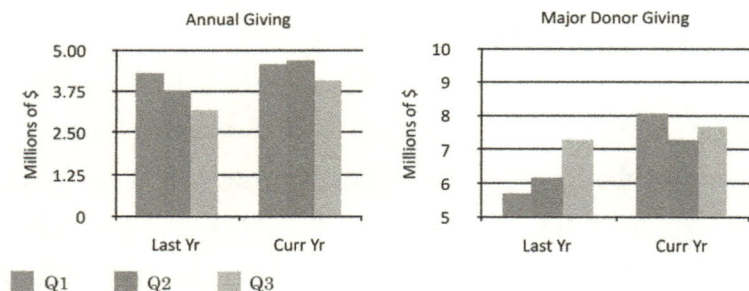

See the problem? At first glance it appears that annual giving has been exceeding major donor giving. But the charts are misleading. The y-axis labels begin at two different places (0 versus 5). Problems like this aren't apparent until people begin comparing graphs in ways they weren't meant to be consumed. Everything was fine until someone put these two charts side by side. Suddenly comparisons are being made across graphs, creating a misleading picture of the data.

So data preparation decisions are critical to the process of developing data-driven strategies. What are we trying to analyze, and what is the best way to depict the data so it can be quickly and accurately understood?

Our analytics team at Pursuant would argue with our data team and tell you that creating graphs that accurately communicate a story is the most challenging part of the process! Perhaps it is. So how do we do that part of the job well?

Let's start by examining some of the basic graph types and what each one does best. As we do, keep in mind that while 100-meter sprinters are typically lousy 1,600-meter runners, that doesn't mean they're lousy athletes. They just have different strengths. The same thing can be said about graphs:

Bar Charts

Bar charts are best for comparing sets of data. The chart at the right does a great job of showing how the figures in each quarter compare to each other over the last three years. Less clear are trends in performance over several years, or even how Q1 performed year over year.

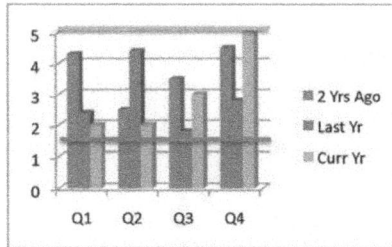

Pie Charts

Pie charts are best for showing proportions or ratios. The pie chart to the right immediately shows that about two-thirds of the year's performance occurs in the first two quarters. By the way, this pie chart is graphing the "Last Yr" figures in the bar chart above. See the difference in perspective?

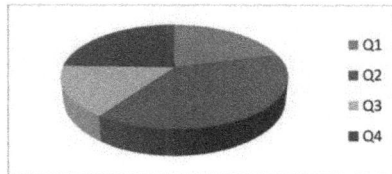

Scatter Plots

Scatter plots are best for viewing groupings of individual data points. The plot to the right shows the number of gifts received at different giving levels. There is a clear indication that more small gifts are being received than large gifts. Plots can be great tools for comparing dissimilar pieces of data.

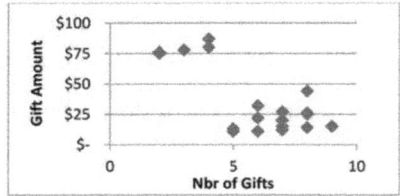

Line Graphs

Line graphs are best for depicting trends over time. Nothing compares to a line graph to show total giving amounts year after year. It may not compare specific periods side by side, but the trend in average gift size (as seen to the right) is very clear. Notice how the last three quarters of Year 3 show a downward trend over prior quarters.

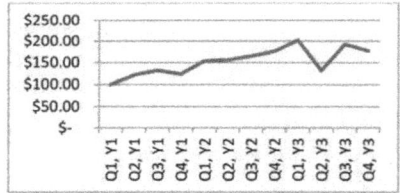

Bubble Plots

Bubble plots are best for comparing three different sets of data. These charts can be complex; but when needed, they put a lot of data into a clear picture. The example here shows a project analysis where Potential Revenue Impact and Level of Difficulty represent the x- and y-axes. The size of the bubbles reflects the cost of each project. Which one would you implement first?

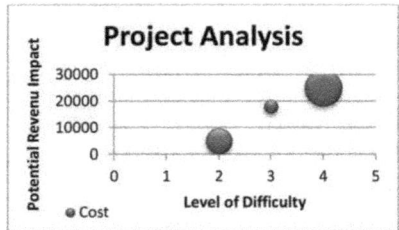

Radar Plots

Also known as "spider plots," radar plots are often used to show areas of strength and weakness. In this example at the right, Actual results show a higher performance in areas such as Planning and Execution, while the Benchmark

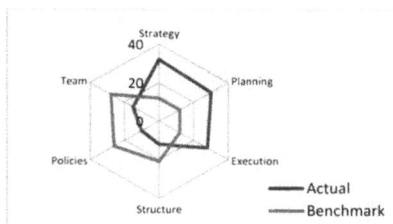

shows better results in the Team and Policies elements. Pursuant uses spider plots extensively in its fundraising and organization assessment instruments.

These charts illustrate the many ways that data can be portrayed, turning tables of forgettable information into interesting, memorable diagrams. But it's critical that analysts first consider what they are trying to depict. Are you comparing sets of data? Trying to show a trend? Are you presenting one hundred data points, or just a few? Are the data points connected in an obvious way, or are they somewhat dissimilar? How many data points need to be graphed?

All of these questions drive the use of different chart forms. It's also important to evaluate how the charts will be used. Are they being presented or printed? With or without commentary? Over what period of time? Is the audience familiar with the data or new to it? How is the intended audience used to seeing the data visualized? How can the visualizations be improved?

Sometimes it helps to add information to a plot, such as trend lines, which show the trajectory of change and eliminate periodic highs and lows. For example, using the line graph example from earlier, I added a linear trend line (at right) to show how the average gift has generally been growing over the last three years. The trend line implies how that data point

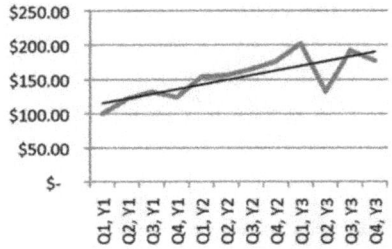

should continue to grow if fundraising efforts prove to be as effective in the future. Today's charting tools make it simple to add different forms of trend lines.

Other additions to charts could include rules that depict information not found on the graph. For example, using the bar chart example from earlier, I added two rules depicting

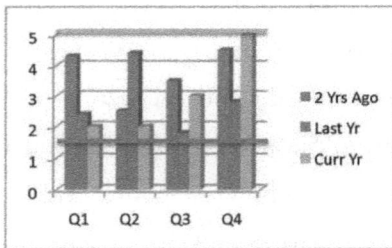

the lowest- and highest-performing quarters in the last five years (see chart at left). How do these rules provide additional context for understanding the data

depicted on this bar chart? Rules like this have a far greater impact than a text note.

One of the most powerful elements in charting—and undoubtedly one of the most challenging—is to consider how combining data points that aren't normally associated with each other can tell an interesting story when they're included on one chart.

For example, Pursuant recently prepared a presentation for a client about their major giving performance. We wanted to see how many of their major donors had given a majority of their gifts in the last three years. Here is what the plot looked like once it was completed:

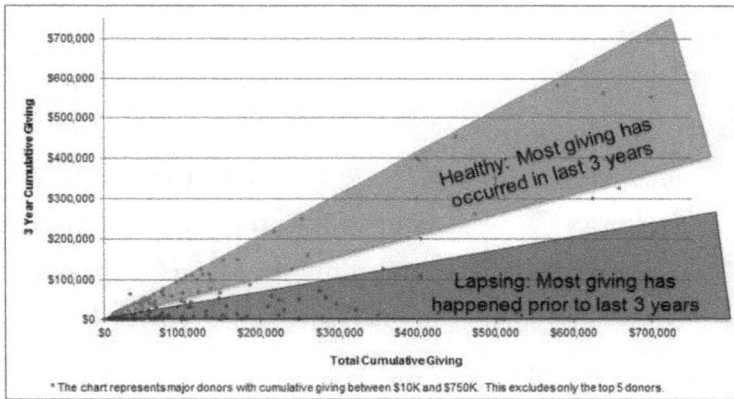

Several things are worth noting about this chart:

1. Notes were added to clarify the critical points.
2. Data on the top five donors were excluded in order to avoid plotting outliers that would have made the chart much more difficult to reach.
3. Highlighted sections were added to show areas of strength and weakness.

The bottom line: This plot was helpful for visualizing the number of donors whose giving had occurred prior to the last three years. While some major donors had done most of their giving in recent years, many others were in the process of lapsing. This created a sense of urgency within the organization to strategize how they might avoid watching a large percentage of their major donors lapse.

Examples like this show the incredible power of visualizing data to help tell a story. Can you imagine the plot just shown depicted in the form of a spreadsheet?

While visualizations are important, they lose their value if poor decisions are made concerning titles, labels, legends, notes, axis lines, fonts, and font sizes and colors.

While visualizations are important, they lose their value if poor decisions are made concerning titles, labels, legends, notes, axis lines, fonts, and font sizes and colors. Popular business charting tools provide an endless array of options for customizing a plot. A person can spend a lot of time adjusting the detailed elements in a series of plots. And some of that time is well spent.

For example, are there brand standards that should be observed in your organization for things such as font styles and color call-outs? How consistent are the colors and fonts used across the graphs and charts in your report or presentation? Does red depict negative information while green is positive? Are labels hard to read because they are depicted in a dark text color against a dark background? Or in a light text color against a light background?

A lack of attention to detail and consistency makes a presentation look sloppy, calling into question both you and the data you're presenting: "If Sam couldn't get the font sizes consistent, then what are the chances that his data are accurate?"

It's impossible to overemphasize the importance of accurate labels, titles, legends, and notes. Every word counts, because text on a chart should be kept to an absolute minimum. In the past I've rewritten chart notes at least twenty times while trying to find an economy of words. I've also been in review meetings where several analysts spent more time than you'd imagine trying to find the right term to use for an x- or y-axis label, or a legend entry, or a title. Words matter—especially when there are very few of them. Use them wisely and also double-check them to make sure they aren't misleading.

> *A lack of attention to detail and consistency makes a presentation look sloppy, calling into question both you and the data you're presenting: "If Sam couldn't get the font sizes consistent, then what are the chances that his data are accurate?"*

It's also vital to consider how the presentation is going to be made. Will it be delivered through a projector? Is it going to be printed? With what level of quality and color? These outcomes should affect any decisions that are made about how the data will be presented.

One final note worth addressing: graphing tools these days offer some very cool options for three-dimensional graphics. It's as easy to select a three-dimensional graph as a two-dimensional one. But be very careful. Sometimes a three-dimensional graph provides visual interest and adds a professional touch to your analytic artwork. But other times it may greatly reduce the clarity of the data and make it virtually unreadable.

Decisions made during the data cleaning and initial presentation stages will set up the next step for success or failure: data immersion.

Data Immersion

The process of deeply understanding data begins once an initial presentation of the data is in place. Pursuant uses dozens and dozens of standard charts and graphs as the starting point for the immersion process. From there, a subject matter expert (SME) takes over the process, looking into the eyes of the data to see the face staring back. Are these donors happy or sad? Are they confused or amazingly responsive? Are they engaging or disengaging?

It's important to bring an objective, unbiased opinion to the process. One of the benefits of analyzing our clients' data is that we have no idea what the process will uncover. If you're looking for something specific, you'll likely "find" it—even if it isn't entirely true. This is no place for jumping to conclusions.

I strongly recommend that you work with a team during this stage. Applying the experiences of different people will make the data immersion process run a lot faster and produce a more complete and accurate outcome in the end.

The first step is to become thoroughly familiar with the data. What is each chart telling you? What is the story behind each graph? If you look at a chart and have no idea if it represents a positive image or a negative one, then it's highly likely that you lack sufficient context to understand the data, much less draw conclusions from it.

During data immersion, themes and general impressions are far more important than any single number. Which data are trending up versus trending down? How does the number compare to the same period in prior years? How does the data change when it's evaluated over quarterly results, or over an entire fiscal year?

Next, what outliers—dramatic peaks or valleys—do you see? How long did the slump last? How recent was the record-setting month? Was the peak twice the norm? Was the dip slight or drastic? This is one of the most important steps in the process. It is critical that you research why the outlier occurred. Look for correlations. What changed during the period in question? Was a specific communication channel or campaign responsible for the unusual decrease or increase? Did an event occur at that same time? Was timing somehow responsible for the change? What else went up or down during that same period?

Contextually speaking, it's important to know what data you're reviewing. Online results? Major giving results? Do the data depict engagement behaviors, such as website visits, click-throughs, or online newsletter registrations? Or do the numbers represent annual/general fund giving data? Or all data? Do they reflect all gifts—including that extraordinary estate gift that came in last year? Do the graphs represent 90 percent of all giving, or only 10 percent of it?

It's also important to have a general sense of industry standards during this process, as it will provide additional context for evaluating the success or failure of a campaign. What was the goal of the campaign? What was budgeted for revenue that month from that catalog mailing or e-mail blast?

Subsector growth and decline represent valuable points of context. An increase in annual giving of 2 percent may seem anemic . . . until you realize that giving to your hospital/health care subsector decreased by 5 percent in the last calendar year. Nonprofit sector and subsector benchmarks are helpful to the immersion and observation process. But keep in mind that every nonprofit has differences that may make overall sector averages less relevant. Don't give them too much weight. They are one data point, but they're not the only data point.

Several years ago I created the following Donor Process Model to help fundraising professionals diagnose fundraising

DONOR PROCESS MODEL

problems. This model highlights eight core areas that will inevitably affect optimal annual giving results:

1. **Impressions:** Too few people are hearing about the work of your organization
2. **Response:** Ineffective tools and techniques for turning impressions into new relationships
3. **Donate:** Poor process for encouraging new people to make an initial gift
4. **Active Donors:** Ineffective communication

that fails to encourage donors to make the all-important second gift to your organization

5. **Renewals:** Ineffective communication that fails to keep donors engaged and supportive over time

6. **Lapsed Donor Reactivation:** Ineffective or nonexistent efforts to encourage lapsed donors to renew their support and become active again

7. **Numbers of Gifts:** Lack of focus on frequent giving programs (or for major donors, a failure to gain support outside of a capital/vision campaign)

8. **Dollar Amount:** A proactive focus on upgrading donors who are ready and willing at higher levels

As you conduct your initial review, consider the different components of the Donor Process Model and how your organization is performing at each step of the process.

Make notes on every page that summarize your initial impressions of each chart and graph. They will become increasingly meaningful as the data immersion process continues. Singular negative trends don't tell the entire story. It's only in the context of the entire picture—sets of observations—that we can begin giving weight and meaning to particular observations.

Once finished, go back through the graphs and your notes. What themes exist across multiple observations? The process of immersion doesn't happen in a single pass. Our SMEs typically have to review the charts and graphs dozens of times while they're creating a mental image of the story that donors are communicating through their giving behaviors.

Undoubtedly you'll need to drill down into the data for more information. Good analytics tools make the process of drilling into data easier. But it's not uncommon to have to conduct additional research and ask for more detailed information on a specific trend.

For example, let's say overall giving was lower than expected in June. Which of the three campaigns that are running that month performed the poorest? What was the problem? The response rate? The average gift size? Was a particular segment unresponsive? Did giving in May "cannibalize" giving in June? Were the donor communications too close together? Was the ask unclear or too soft? Was the need not well represented? Was the story not compelling? Or did the communication arrive too late to drive support for that month?

Answering these questions will begin to give you clarity about what needs to change in order to improve future results. The donor development process is one that involves constantly asking questions and learning what worked and what didn't work.

I once worked with an organization that discovered that every day they were late on an appeal mailing, it translated into a five-figure impact on giving. That single statistic made an indelible impression on the organization's leaders and highlighted the true cost of taking an extra day to make a subtle wording change on their donor appeal letters!

The goal of immersion is to gain clarity on the most important issues impacting donor engagement and financial support. Giving may be going down, but understanding the causes of decreased giving will have everything to do with discovering the necessary strategies for turning the trend in a positive direction.

Consider the following scenarios—all of which Pursuant has observed in various client engagements:

- Lack of a compelling story or a poor case for support
- Communications spaced too close together or too far apart
- Decreases in giving to the subsector
- Lack of investment in/attention to donor acquisition over the last X years
- Lack of engagement with new prospective donors
- Poor process for connecting with major donors in a meaningful, personal way

- Lack of expertise among the staff responsible for cultivating certain levels of support
- Unclear e-mail copy or poor design
- Website landing pages that are too complex
- Costs that are unnecessarily high
- Ineffective reengagement of lapsed donors
- Unclear or nonexistent call to action
- Donor fatigue from either too much "urgency" or a general lack of urgency

Remember: Prescribing changes in fundraising efforts without first conducting a proper diagnosis is tantamount to committing fundraising malpractice.

Now that you're armed with a distinct set of clear, supportable observations and root causes, you are ready to move to the final stage of the process: developing data-driven strategies.

> *Remember: Prescribing changes in fundraising efforts without first conducting a proper diagnosis is tantamount to committing fundraising malpractice.*

Data-Driven Strategies

If you've done the job properly in the earlier stages, then creating effective strategies to respond to your observations will be the easiest part of the process. Note your primary (approximately three to five) observations. Which charts and graphs do the best job of visualizing the problems or opportunities for growth or improvement? Those visuals need to be placed front and center in the presentation of results. What do you want your staff to remember?

The rest of your graphs should become part of the appendix to your report. It isn't that they're unimportant; they just aren't necessary for focusing attention on the primary areas of need. Don't marginalize your hard work by trying to impress people with all of the data you reviewed while coming to your conclusions.

Strategies should quickly emerge. If the problem is acquisition, where can you find prospective donors? How do we educate them about the work of our organization? How can we do that in a way that's interesting and perhaps even entertaining? How might we engage the power of our existing donors in telling our story to their networks of friends? How can we make that process easy and enjoyable?

Pursuant has found the use of online "edutainment" campaigns (combining education and entertainment) to be an incredible means for creating a "viral" acquisition process where more people respond to an invitation than were initially invited to participate. Social media is great for this kind of approach.

What incentives might you provide to encourage donors to participate? Why should they share your story with others? What would make it worth their while? How can you create a process for engagement that reduces the friction commonly associated with engagement? These are questions that a strategist can help you answer, and they are the secret to creating strong, effective acquisition campaigns.

If your problem is keeping donors engaged, consider how your communication efforts should be changed to create excitement and appreciation for your work. Effective storytelling, perhaps through the use of compelling video messages, can have a dramatic impact on people. We live in a world of video communication. Video creates a vicarious experience for people to see firsthand the impact of your transformational work.

I encourage you to consider your organization's vision as well. If your most significant goals require double-digit growth, then developing strategies that create incremental improvement will be insufficient for getting you where you want and need to go. You have to get aggressive. Develop strategies that will engage thousands of donors. Reengaging lapsed donors or increasing the average gift of donors by 2 to 5 percent may be worthy objectives. But they're insufficient for organizations that need to drive annual growth into the 20 percent range.

In our experience at Pursuant, viral acquisition and engagement programs, aggressive mid-level donor upgrading strategies, and large capital/vision campaigns offer that kind of growth potential. General donor cultivation efforts are extremely important to sustaining donor support over time. They form the foundation for any comprehensive fundraising program.

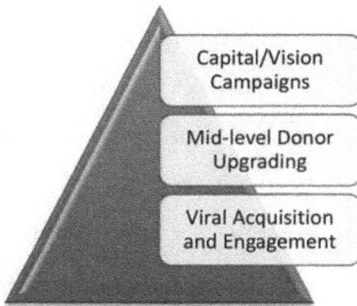

But high-growth trajectories require injecting a lot more gas into the engine, and potentially at multiple levels of the donor pyramid. Strongly consider how these three strategies might be leveraged to drive considerable growth across your entire donor file.

Capital/Vision Campaigns

Mid-level Donor Upgrading

Viral Acquisition and Engagement

It's also important that you construct a return on investment (ROI) projection for each strategy. Most initiatives will require some kind of incremental investment. After all, it takes money to raise money. Develop some simple projections for both cost and the anticipated revenue that will be generated by the initiative. For example, how would acquiring an additional ten thousand donors affect giving over the next three years? How would an increase in donor retention improve giving results over three years? Doing both will have an exponential impact on total giving.

Don't consider the cost alone. Look at revenue and cost. Is there a major donor who'd be willing to support an expanded fundraising effort? Most major donors love knowing that the impact of their gift will result in even greater levels of giving. In effect, their gift becomes a "challenge grant" that generates giving from other untapped areas of support.

Finally, consider the sequencing of your new strategies. Which initiatives should be implemented first? Just because an initiative will produce the greatest or most immediate financial impact, that doesn't necessarily make it the highest priority. Your institution may be best served by driving mid-level support first, followed in two or three years by a capital campaign that can take advantage of a new, much larger pool of mid-level donors who will then be ready to respond. Determining the right sequence of strategies is as important as identifying the strategies themselves.

Conclusion

Too many chief development officers jump headlong into programs that may have worked in their former lives, but no longer represent the best investment for the organizations they currently serve. Taking a measured, data-driven approach will ensure that your investment in capturing "big data" produces returns that can make a material difference in your fundraising results.

Turning big data into donor support is a considerable but critical undertaking for any nonprofit organization seeking to maximize growth in top line revenue. Done well, the creation of a comprehensive, strategic fundraising plan will be one of the best investments you can make toward sustainable support . . . and the transformational impact that sits at the core of your nonprofit enterprise.

Let us know how we can help. We realize that your staff are extremely busy meeting the daily fundraising needs of your organization. Therefore, Pursuant has developed a cost-effective, turnkey approach to not only analyzing our clients' significant data stores and fundraising campaigns, but also turning our observations into comprehensive strategic fundraising plans that are appropriate to your organization's unique situation and revenue needs.

We would love to partner with you in identifying some visionary strategies that will transform your big data into donor intelligence that drives lasting support.

But before we can talk about visionary *strategies*, you had better understand and be able to define your *vision*. That's what we'll look at in the next chapter.

6

I Have a Dream:
The Importance of Vision

TRENT RICKER

This chapter uses two famous "dream" speeches to illustrate the power of sharing a precise and simple vision with your donors. Your vision should tell the story of your organization's priorities and ultimately take your donors on a journey that recognizes each gift as their participation in helping bring to fruition the organization's vision and multiyear goals.

Vision and the Capital Campaign

As fundraisers, we are most familiar—and often most comfortable—defining vision related to a campaign. A campaign forces us to draw donors into our organization's vision. We are compelled to articulate a clear case for support that is inspirational, identifies needs and threats, and provides simply stated tangible outcomes to achieve in a defined time frame. That's vision. We do it for campaigns; unfortunately we're not typically doing it elsewhere. In that way, campaigns have become a vision crutch.

We Are Losing Sight of Our Vision

Oftentimes organizations have disconnected goals and lack a sense of direction. Sometimes there's a real chasm between mission, core purpose, and day-to-day activities. Often that's because there is *a lot going on*. We have strategic initiatives, plans, activities, and individual goals that we're all trying to achieve—whether it's meeting a revenue number on the same budget as last year or maintaining a certain ROI in the midst of budget reductions. Bottom line, the metrics, measures, and responsibilities of our job day to day bog us down and create a chasm between our mission, our core values, why we exist, and who we serve. We are focused on goals and initiatives but lose sight of the larger vision.

What Is Vision?

Fundamentally, vision inspires. The great Dr. Martin Luther King Jr. was obviously an incredible visionary, perhaps the greatest of the twentieth century. His famous "I Have a Dream" speech inspired an entire nation and multiple generations toward a very powerful movement. His vision was raw and bold, and he believed in it deeply. His speech provides examples of things that are essential to communicating vision.

What is Vision?

I have a dream...

✓ that one day, down in **Alabama**, with its vicious racists... right there in Alabama little black boys and black girls **will be able to join hands** with little white boys and white girls as sisters and brothers.

✓ that one day on the red hills of **Georgia**, the sons of former slaves and the sons of former slave owners **will be able to sit down together** at the table of brotherhood.

✓ that **my four little children will one day live** in a nation where they **will not be judged by the color of their skin but by the content of their character**.

- **Real Places:** He talked about Alabama and Georgia—real places where real people live.
- **Concrete Outcomes:** He shared real outcomes—when he saw specific things begin to happen, it would be an indicator of his vision being fulfilled.
- **Timeline:** He put his vision in the context of time. He wanted these things to happen in his children's lifetime.

JFK's "Man on the Moon" Speech

✓ First, I believe that this nation should commit itself to achieving the goal, **before this decade is out**, of **landing a man on the Moon and returning him safely to the Earth.**

✓ Secondly, an **additional 23 million dollars,** together with 7 million dollars already available, **will accelerate development of the Rover nuclear rocket.**

✓ Third, an **additional 50 million dollars** will make the most of our present leadership, by **accelerating the use of space satellites for world-wide communications.**

✓ Fourth, an **additional 75 million dollars**--of which 53 million dollars is for the Weather Bureau--will help give us at the earliest possible time **a satellite system for world-wide weather observation.**

Another great luminary from the 1960s, President John F. Kennedy, provides an even better example of establishing vision over a period of time. His famous and powerful "Man on the Moon" speech to Congress set the vision for the Space Age. It is one of the best examples of a vision statement out there.

- **Clear Timeline**—"before this decade is out"
- **Simple Goal**—"land a man on the moon and return him safely"
- **Stated Priorities**—concrete numbers and an explanation of how funds would be allocated

JFK's "Man on the Moon" Speech

Let it be clear ... that I am asking the Congress and the country to accept a firm commitment to a new course of action – **a course which will last for many years and carry heavy costs**: 531 million dollars in fiscal '62 – an estimated seven to nine billion dollars additional over the next five years.

If we are to go only half way, or reduce our sights in the face of difficulty, in my judgment it would be better not to go at all.

The last thing JFK did was make it clear that achieving the vision wouldn't be easy; it was a bold vision. It was a course that would last for many years and carry very heavy costs.

- **Acknowledged Difficulty**—he prepared people for a real challenge that would require sacrifice and total commitment

He clarified that we cannot do this halfway; otherwise we're better off having never tried. That's compelling. It challenges people. It helps them understand that they need to be involved in the long term and not follow half measures.

The Seven Aspects Your Vision Needs

1. **Your vision should establish the need and the threat.** The first thing JFK talked about is why it is important to put a man on the moon, along with the threat of Soviet dominance in this arena. A vision needs to establish need and threat first.

2. **Your vision should be inspirational and transformational.** It must cause people to want to stand up, applaud, and say, "I want to be a part of that."

3. **Your vision must have simply stated, tangible outcomes.** Anyone should be able to understand it in the moment.

Your vision should be inspirational and transformational. It must cause people to want to stand up, applaud, and say, "I want to be a part of that."

4. **Your vision needs defined time horizons.** There needs to be accountability regarding when we will arrive at the destination.

5. **Your vision should have clearly articulated requirements.** JFK's speech gave strict dollar amounts.

6. **Your vision must be bold and require sacrifice.** When people are asked to sacrifice for something bold that they believe in, it's incredibly powerful, and it renders a deep level of commitment to the organization.

7. **Your vision must not settle for half measures.** If you and the donor believe in the vision, neither of you should settle for second best.

Recognizing Vision-Absent Fundraising

If you look around, you'll notice a lot of vision-absent fundraising. It's not always bad fundraising, but it's generally transactional rather than visionary.

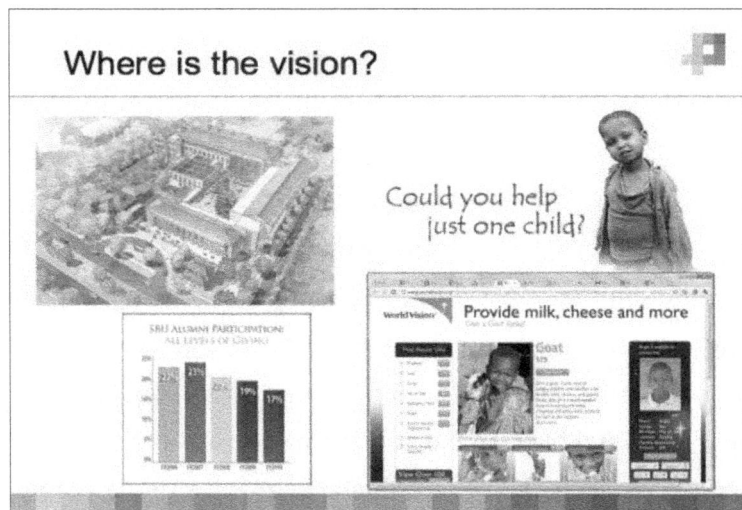

There are four types of vision-absent fundraising. Child/animal sponsorships are a wonderful fundraising tactic, but from a fundraising perspective, sponsorships are transactional. The donor doesn't see beyond the individual gift. The vision is absent.

Buildings are an excellent way to raise money. Putting a blueprint or artist's rendering in front of a donor is pretty powerful. People get excited, but it's not visionary fundraising. Without a discussion of how it will affect people's lives, buildings are very organization-centric. What if JFK had only shown a blueprint of Cape Canaveral and said, "We're going to build a great rocket pad"? What would be the point? The rocket pad exists to take people to the moon. We need to remember the outcomes in our vision.

Gift catalogs are a wonderful device that a lot of organizations use to allow people to buy alternative gifts to help someone out. But again, a gift catalog does not speak to the overall vision of the organization, but rather, the onetime gift.

Finally, **participation appeals**, which are all too common in higher education, are almost never an effective approach because most donors don't care that much about participation. Further, participation appeals are so organization-centric—lacking any conversation about how lives are affected—that they aren't going to connect with the donor.

Transactional Fundraising

If used exclusively, transactional fundraising can add to donor churn because it's acquisition-oriented rather than retention-oriented. While you might use a transactional tactic up front to encourage the first gift, it's important to infuse vision as early as possible to help produce a long-term relationship. We must invite the donor to go on a journey with us. Doing so will align the donor's passions with your organization and inspire them to want to be part of something bigger.

Reasons Donors Make a Second Gift

In May/June 2011, the Association of Fundraising Professionals conducted a study on why donors make a second gift. The top answer—76 percent of respondents said *the organization explained a specific mission*. It's about putting the vision into context for donors and telling them why we do what we do and where we are going. It gives the donor a chance to say, "Okay. Great. I want to be a part of that." And that makes a huge difference going forward.

The Campaign Arc

If we look at donor engagement with a capital campaign, it resembles an arc. Campaigns begin with a *preparation phase*— planning studies, feasibility studies, talking to potential leadership and potential donors, forming a cabinet, and so forth. Then there's the *quiet phase*, where you're trying to raise a large bulk of the money from your largest donors; then you draw everybody in for the *public phase*; and finally, at the end is the *celebration*.

A campaign invites different types of people in during the different elements of the campaign. Obviously lead donors come in early and give those big gifts; then they

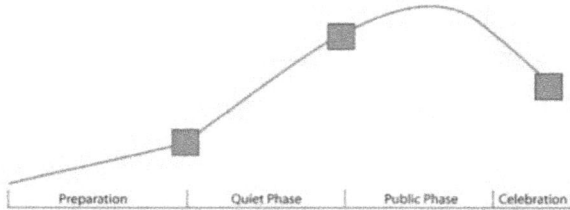

Vision Development

Campaigns have clearly defined structures:

| Preparation | Quiet Phase | Public Phase | Celebration |

become advocates in helping promote your campaign. At the very end you have smaller donors coming in, and they're helping to round out the campaign for the big celebration.

The Storytelling Arc

The campaign arc closely resembles the story arc of most films, three-act plays, and even twenty-minute TV sitcoms. Beginning with act I, characters are introduced. In act II, the obstacle arises. The final conflict shows up in act III, and the denouement draws everything together to resolution.

Using the JFK example, in act I he made his speech and asked for financing. "We're going to put a man on the moon by the end of the decade and bring him back safely." In act II, they were building the rockets, testing the vehicles, trying to get a man into space—all clear reasons

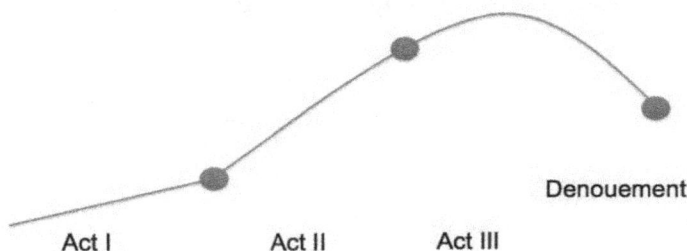

Vision-Infused Fundraising

A structure much like your favorite movie:

Denouement

Act I   Act II   Act III

for needing support. Moving into act III, astronauts are orbiting the moon, and everyone witnessed that milestone. Obviously the payoff shows up at the end, in the conclusion, as the outcome is multiple moon landings. As it relates to fundraising, when we invite donors on these types of journeys, we're setting ourselves up to encourage further engagement with them philanthropically, over time, in multiple areas as the story unfolds.

Vision-Infused Fundraising

This arc gives us a model for how to share our organization's vision with donors. When your overarching vision (story) infuses everything you do—campaign or not—it allows donors to participate throughout the entire process and participate more than once. At every level along that journey,

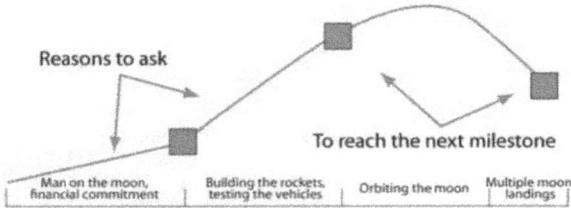

Vision Development

Fundraising with vision is simply to have the ability to tell your story over time. **Invite your donor on a journey that is bigger than the next ask*.**

Reasons to ask

To reach the next milestone

| Man on the moon, financial commitment | Building the rockets, testing the vehicles | Orbiting the moon | Multiple moon landings |

we want to invite donors into the narrative. When they see how the journey affects lives, it becomes something they want to be a part of for the long term. And every time we hit a milestone, we have another reason to come back, make another ask, and involve them again in the story.

Like JFK's speech, true vision includes milestones of different priorities so donors understand their role doesn't end at just one gift. This doesn't apply only to major donors; it also applies to the person who thinks, *I've done my part*, after giving $50 to buy a goat for a family in Africa. In either case, we end up going back and asking again: "Well, the need's still there; can you give another goat for another $50?" Alternatively, when you lay out the vision from the outset with clarity about what will be involved, that there are phases and milestones to accomplish and that they will need to be involved again—that's a compelling vision. Because we all want to be part of something bigger.

What Vision Is Not

As you consider what the story/vision/journey is for your organization, there are a few key things to keep in mind:

Vision is not about being number one. Wanting to be "the best" is not a very compelling vision. A vision should be about a destination that you're trying to reach that has some sort of impact on people's lives.

Vision is not about rankings. Rankings can hold us hostage, especially for higher education and health care institutions. Being tier one, tier two, tier three, top fifty, or top twenty is helpful for marketing or recruiting. But a ranking is not a vision for a donor; it says nothing about how a life has changed or how someone is affected. My colleague Gary Cole always says, "Donors don't want to help organizations; they want to help the people that organizations want to help." If you're too focused on yourself, or your rankings, you're going to fundamentally miss what will connect a donor to your organization.

> *"Donors don't want to help organizations; they want to help the people that organizations want to help."*
> *—Gary Cole*

Vision is not a dollar goal. Fundraising goals and other metrics may be interesting to fundraisers, but a dollar goal is not going to inspire a donor. Especially as you move down the donor pyramid and try to engage all levels of your donor base, the more you emphasize a dollar goal, the more insignificant donors start to feel at the mid-level and at the lower levels. Their gift is just a drop in the bucket of your tremendous goal. Instead of fundraising goals, focus on the real impact of the organization and connect your donor to helping you achieve something that is fundamentally inspiring.

Vision in Practice

Using the example President Kennedy provided, a man on the moon and back safely was the overarching vision, with several other priorities that came under it. That was the inspirational part folks could really get behind. His additional priorities weren't all directly related to putting a man on the moon.

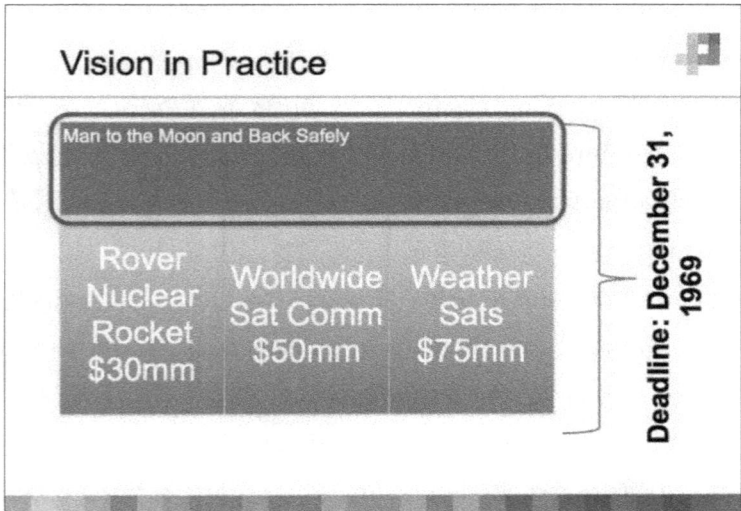

Vision in Practice

Man to the Moon and Back Safely

Rover Nuclear Rocket $30mm | Worldwide Sat Comm $50mm | Weather Sats $75mm

Deadline: December 31, 1969

When you're setting a vision, your related concepts can feed into the vision, but they don't have to be directly related to it.

A lot of campaigns, and even visions, do a great job of pinning down the top three to four priorities, but miss the opportunity to define a simple, inspirational concept to communicate the vision. Instead, they use generalities: "We want our college to be the best," "We want our hospital to be best," or "We want our organization to help alleviate poverty." These are all wonderful goals. But in the headline, we must also have one succinct and simple sentence to which someone can respond, "Yes, I want to be part of that."

Your vision should be reviewed annually to ensure it still fits the direction of your organization.

Vision Is Not Branding

Oftentimes, we do a good job with branding and logos/visual identities, but branding is not the same as vision. Branding a vision is not the same as a simple-to-understand statement like, "Send a man to the moon and back safely." Vision raises our eyes higher, beyond just simple priorities, and gives us something to believe in.

Vision Is Not Mission

Mission is what you do. That doesn't change over time for most organizations. It will likely be the same fifty years from now. But vision will shift regularly. Vision statements should be revised every five to ten years—a time frame that is measurable and tangible. And even within that five- to ten-year time frame, your vision should be reviewed annually to ensure it still fits the direction of your organization.

Creating Your Own Vision

Modeling after JFK's vision and priorities, an organization's vision might look something like this.

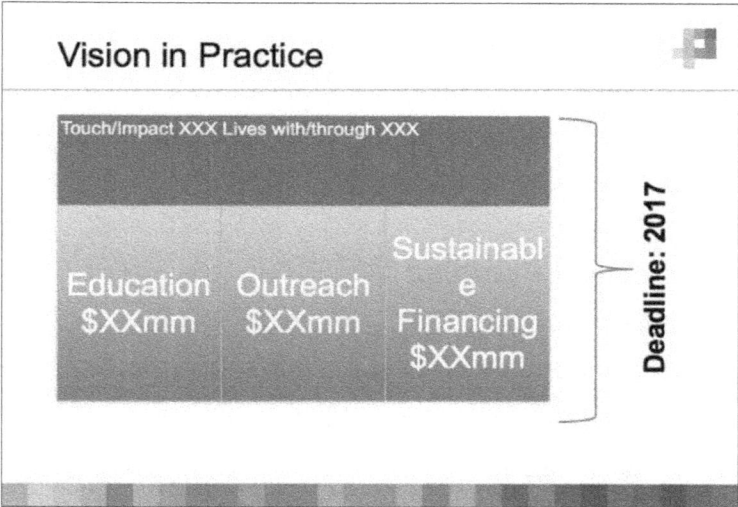

Specify how it would define, touch, or influence a certain number of lives, with or through some particular channel, medium, or programmatic method. Then, underneath, specify priorities with a firm deadline.

How Does This Help Tactically?

Here are just a few benefits of connecting different types of donors with your compelling vision:

Major/Mid-Level Donors. Setting a progressive vision using the story arc allows each ask to act as a milestone as the vision is accomplished. It allows you to go back and say, "Thanks! We got to step 1 because of you. Now, we need to go to step 2 together." If your organization does a lot of campaigns, it also transcends the campaign and allows you to go back to make asks outside the campaign currently in place.

Annual Donors. A clear vision makes planning direct mail and online messaging easy. You've already defined the language of your priorities and vision, which provides a blueprint for direct-response activities. As donors move on the journey with you, it also provides compelling reasons for people to upgrade their giving from $100 to $500 and from $500 to $1,500 based on the progress you're making toward this vision. It provides context, and donors will feel as if they're on a journey. It's not just another transactional ask.

New Donors. Having a strong vision provides easy, compelling context for a welcome series as you steward and cultivate donors toward a second gift. It's a natural segue to the second ask—a way to say, "Join us on this journey toward this vision."

Planned Givers. With planned-giving donors, it's all about their legacy—their philanthropic vision of what they want to commit to and how they want to be remembered. A strong vision allows you to align their priorities with the organization's priorities. It also provides a broader context. As you're moving toward your vision, illustrate how donors' loved ones left behind can engage to see this vision come to fruition.

Prospects. Use your vision to engage people's imagination. Invite them somewhere compelling, and give them an incentive to be a part of something bigger.

Vision Is Bigger Than Any Campaign

Unlike a campaign, which may have just a few leaders engaged, bringing in others only as necessary, a vision is shared across the entire organization all the time. When the leadership and board embrace and champion everyone's participation in the vision, it becomes the foundation of everything you do. Everyone is responsible for it in equal measure, because a vision is about where the organization is going. From development and advancement, programs and services, operations and administration—everyone has a part to play and is focused on meeting that same vision.

That's when you start to see unified messaging. There ceases to be conflict over when messaging goes out, who owns it, who is sending to the e-mail list, who's supposed to be on the Facebook page, or who's tweeting. It begins to be

Vision is Bigger Than Any Campaign

Programs / Services

Development / Advancement

Operations / Administration

Board

Shared Vision

Leadership

Participation in and **Responsibility** for a Vision is **shared equally** across the entire organization

Unified Messaging

unified because the messaging is all about the vision. There might be some different sub-messages, but if everyone is all about the vision, then the goals are aligned.

Donors will start to hear about that vision, even when it's not a fundraising ask, and they'll relate back to it and know exactly what's being talked about. They'll almost be stewarded throughout that process, because you're on a unified path as an organization toward it. Having a bold vision helps us begin to eliminate the risk and fear of donors receiving mixed messages.

A Challenge

Take a look at your organization's strategic plan, case for support, mission statement, or even your current vision statement—review them all. Then ask yourself, "What could we achieve by the end of the decade? How could we impact lives through our mission, through our community, in our nation, or in the world?"

What Is Your Man-on-the-Moon Concept?

Next, write your own "I Have a Dream"/"Man on the Moon" speech, just one or two pages, defining that compelling concept or one sentence that would make people say, "I want to get on board!" Start by thinking about what makes YOU passionate about your organization. Why are you fundraising for it? Then write out some of those principles and priorities. Focus on concrete statements of impact that you will have over time. You may not have access to exact numbers. That's okay; begin to think it through anyway. That one sentence, the elevator pitch of your vision, should be so simple and so compelling that anyone can grasp it right away.

Then Share It

Once you have a draft, circulate it internally. See if it gets people thinking. Share it with leadership, or if you're in leadership, share it with the board. Share it in a manner that begins a conversation about putting this structure in place for your organization. Because when you do, it can revolutionize your fundraising and energize your donor base.

Remember Your Dream

Dreaming connects us to the things that are important to us. Dr. Martin Luther King Jr. had a dream. President Kennedy had a dream. Both dreams were bigger than any one man could accomplish, and yet they weren't too big for an entire nation to take hold of. What is your dream for your organization? What inspires you to come to work every day? What are the stories that take hold of your heart and make you glad you are on this journey? That's exactly what your donors need to hear in your vision. Using the clearly articulated examples from these two speeches, find your way to a succinct vision that will take your donors on a journey and compel them to want to partner with you for a lifetime.

7

Redefining Fundraising

CURT SWINDOLL

Several years ago, I served in a fundraising capacity for a nonprofit. After some time on the job, I was curious if my three kids knew what I did for a living. So I asked them.

Their response: "You have lunch and dinner with people."

Their answer highlights the essence of a foundational problem in the fundraising arena: a tendency to focus on tactics.

Fundraising is a discipline—one documented in academic research and literature, one that is supported through extensive consultative and training services, and one that should be practiced by professionals who have studied the art and science behind what it takes to successfully raise funds for nonprofit mission and vision purposes.

But some fundraising programs suffer from the leadership of fundraisers who are new to their positions. In the absence of experience and knowledge, they replicate the tactics of their predecessors or of other nonprofit organizations who may very well be functioning the same way.

The field of fundraising is hardly alone in this respect. Companies routinely ask people to lead and serve in areas where they don't know what they don't know.

To be clear, there are many outstanding fundraising professionals in our field serving worthy nonprofit organizations. To them, this chapter may simply offer an important reminder: that fundraising should be driven from a data-based, strategic perspective, not a tactical one.

For others who are newer to the profession, my hope is that this chapter challenges you to redefine fundraising. Nonprofit missions need quality support and professional leadership.

What is involved in diagnosing an organization's donor development challenges? How does diagnosis inform a comprehensive strategy? How is strategy executed? I hope this chapter can shed some light on these important questions and provide input for those seeking a deeper understanding of how to construct a strong, comprehensive fundraising program, one that really works for their organization.

The Problem

Greg Mortenson is best known for his best-selling book *Three Cups of Tea* (New York: Viking Penguin, 2006). But no one knew who he was back in 1993 when he first started trying to raise funds to provide educational programs to young girls in Pakistan. His first attempts at fundraising were a complete failure. He sent 580 letters to celebrities, businesspeople, and popular Americans and received one response from Tom Brokaw for $100. He wrote sixteen grant requests, every one of which was rejected.[1]

Mr. Mortenson ran headlong into the same problem faced by many nonprofits. We take what is familiar and craft a strategy around it. We discover a technique that works, and then continue the cycle by repeating the newfound tactic. If direct mail proves to be a successful way to connect with donors willing to give, we send more mail. If running major donor events or capital campaigns was helpful, then that becomes our focus.

What began as a single tactic becomes the centerpiece of our strategic plan, even if we didn't fully understand what made it "work" in the first place. But the plan says, "Do it again," further cementing the practice as a staple in our fundraising diet.

In time, we build an ecosystem around the tactic by hiring staff who write direct response letters, craft compelling videos, design beautiful websites, or plan memorable events. In the process, we institutionalize our fundraising strategy around specific creative capabilities, but with little strategic

---

1   Kevin Fedarko, "He Fights Terror with Books," *Parade* magazine, April 6, 2003, http://archive.today/xuolg.

understanding or thought. Our tactic informs our strategy instead of using a robust, data-driven strategic planning process to inform a balanced and comprehensive suite of practices.

Unfortunately, most fundraising consultancies operate the same way. Too many direct response consultants will tell you that your funding needs can be solved through printed letters and postage stamps. Website design firms tell you a new site will cure your communication and donor connection concerns. They have creative strengths. They do that work well, so it's understandable that they are going to try to sell those specific services in the form of a solution.

Is it wrong to capitalize on a strength? Of course not. But if we aren't careful, strengths cause us to miss opportunities to connect in new ways with new constituents.

Is it wrong to capitalize on a strength? Of course not. But if we aren't careful, strengths cause us to miss opportunities to connect in new ways with new constituents, or to enhance what was once a strategic strength but has been weakened over time through almost mindless repetition.

So how do we break the cycle where tactics drive strategies, which in turn drive the same tactics and strategies over and over? We redefine the fundraising strategic planning process.

Data

The knowledge industry has been touting for some time that great decisions come from great data. They call it the DIKW model.[2] The model shows that data, given context, becomes information. Information, given meaning, becomes knowledge. Knowledge, given insight, becomes wisdom. And wisdom, when combined with purpose, results in great decisions and strategic plans.

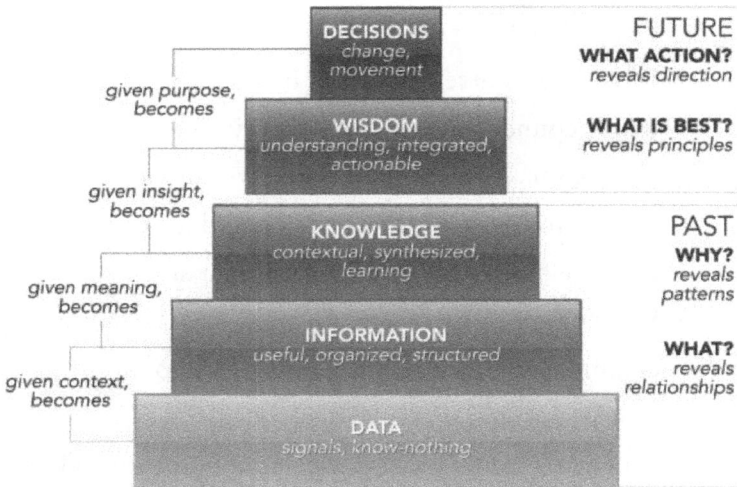

So clearly, if we desire to make better strategic decisions about how we connect with donors and build relationships, we need to begin with data.

---

2   See http://www.systems-thinking.org/dikw/dikw.htm and many other web sources for more information.

But what kind of data? Virtually any piece of information about our donors and the environment in which we are collectively operating could be important.

A Few Questions Pursuant Uses in the Discovery Process

- What is the organization's mission and vision (3–5 years out)? Who finds the mission and vision compelling?
- What is the current state of the fundraising and donor connection process? Historically, how has the organization communicated with donors and prospective donors? How consistent has it been? How well have they been telling their story?
- What channels of communication have been used to communicate: face-to-face, mail, telephone, events, website, e-mail, social media?
- Where are donors and prospects congregating? How do they communicate? Who do they respect?
- What are the points of pain? The organization's needs and desires?
- What do they know about their donors—their profile, demographics, giving history, activities, responsiveness, preferences, engagement areas, and much more?

- What do we know about the environment? What other nonprofits are offering similar services? How does the organization differentiate itself from everyone else, thereby making the donor's decision for support an easy one to make?
- What is the actual experience of people when they contact the organization? For the first time? With a gift or an order? With a need? Online?

Leading nonprofits don't just ask these questions of themselves. They seek input from their donors. Research projects that delve into the perceptions and motivations of potential, current, and lapsed donors can offer invaluable direction in how an organization should frame its message to constituents. When this data is used to drive more effective communication, giving has increased by 60 percent or more.

There is no substitute for comprehensive, accurate data, organized into useful information that can be synthesized into actionable knowledge and wisdom. It is the starting point of building and executing a solid fundraising strategy.

DATA	PHILOSOPHY	STRATEGY	CREATIVE	RESULTS
donor intel research environment	Pursuant Way experience training	direction messages channels	counsel development execution	response trends ROI

Data: The First Element

Data becomes the first element in a five-step process for creating and executing a comprehensive, effective donor development plan. But where do you find the meaning and insight needed to turn information into actionable, strategic decisions? The answer has everything to do with your philosophy of fundraising.

Philosophy

Turning data into knowledge and wisdom comes through a filtering and synthesis process. The meaning and insight we need to translate information into actionable knowledge and wisdom come from experience and education. Wisdom and knowledge inform your philosophy of fundraising. Even intuition, the pre-rational interpretation of a situation that gives us a sense or inclination about how to respond to it, is essentially the leveraging of deeply engrained experience. The less experience or education we have, the less we should rely on our intuition to drive strategic decisions.

> *The less experience or education we have, the less we should rely on our intuition to drive strategic decisions.*

A CPA friend of mine once challenged me to see the "face" looking up at me from a financial statement. His encouragement is the perfect application of this principle. Financial transactions, even if organized into an information-rich, well-structured financial statement, mean nothing without corresponding experience in reading financials or training in finance. The relationship (or ratio) of assets to liabilities, the relative levels of functional (administrative, fundraising, and program) expenses, and debt ratios are all meaningless without an informed, well-rounded financial philosophy.

Regrettably, many fundraising professionals and consultants lack experience and education in significant cross-sections of the donor development landscape. They have worked narrowly in the channels of direct mail, digital development, or capital campaigns. They have been exposed to sections of the donor pyramid, such as lower-tier, annual fund work at a university. But they lack the breadth and depth of experience critical to crafting a comprehensive fundraising strategy that crosses all channels of communication and touches all levels of the donor pyramid.

In short, they may see a page of donor statistics, but they lack the experience needed to see the faces of their donors looking up at them.

Instead, their experience has informed what equates to a lopsided philosophy that capitalizes on certain practices while discounting others. They may have ample data telling them their direct mail is excluding "Gen Y" donors. Their statistics may scream for a social media campaign or a mobile application that engages volunteers. But their incomplete philosophy makes it impossible to see. To help combat blindsides, it is important to document a comprehensive philosophy that articulates your foundational beliefs about donor development and relationship development.

The Donor Development Process Model pictured on the next page encourages a more in-depth evaluation of the fundraising practices by highlighting variables critical to success. It also communicates to staff that the organization values fundraising within the context of a relationship development process.

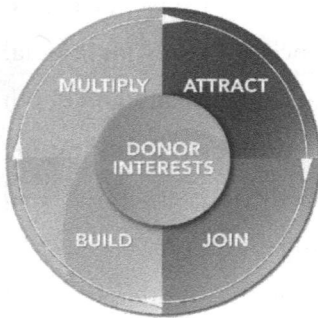

The Pursuant Paradigm: Driving the Relationship Cycle

Models, such as the Pursuant Paradigm pictured left , communicate core beliefs concerning the stages of donor relationship development and key strategies important at each point of development.

It prompts the questions: Where are we struggling? How well are we encouraging people who are attracted to us into joining, or activating, their relationship with us? Are our deepest relationships being used to multiply the impact of our organization and attract new connections to our cause?

Donor Development Process Model

Fundraising professionals use models like these to identify holes in their donor development system, and then use those observations to drive strategic program changes and additions. But the evaluation process goes much deeper than that.

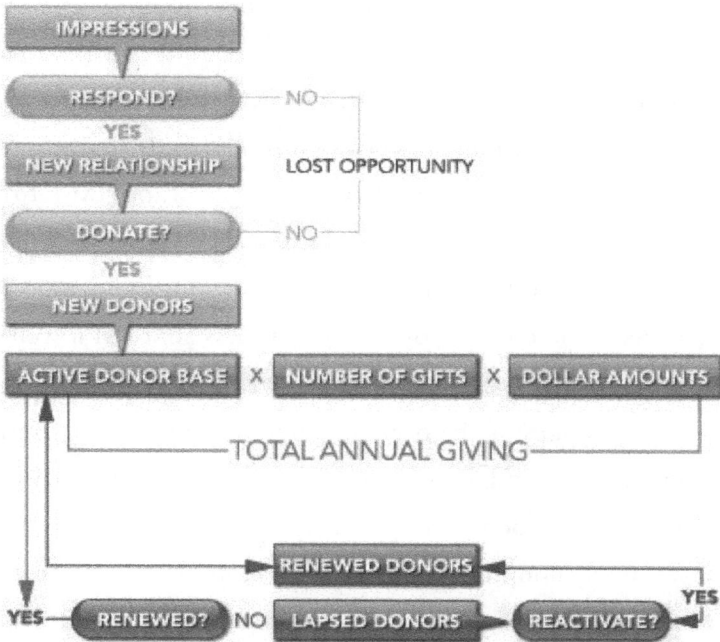

This model identifies seven areas, any one of which can hurt annual giving results over time:

1. The number of marketplace impressions
2. The rate of response to impressions
3. The conversion or activation of new relationships
4. The rate of retention as relationships are built over time

5. The ability to renew relationships with those who have grown distant

6. The frequency of giving from committed donors

7. The level of giving from committed donors

The communication channels diagram pictured on the next page reminds fundraising professionals that many forms of communication exist and are important for disseminating an organization's core messages: what they do, why it is important, and how well it is working. This model also reflects the connection these channels share in a well-crafted fundraising system. Not only are they connected to the core messages of the organization, but the ring pictured in the background is a reminder that communication channels need to be interconnected.

Yet many nonprofits manage the communication process via functional or constituent-based silos. Major gift officers don't talk to annual fund directors, and those groups often fail to coordinate their communication plans with the web development, direct mail, and newsletter teams. In larger organizations, these groups often work in different buildings under different group leaders.

Is it any wonder our communication efforts are fragmented? Who is tying these communication campaigns together? Do we think major donors don't read newsletters, or that event participants won't be concerned if our websites

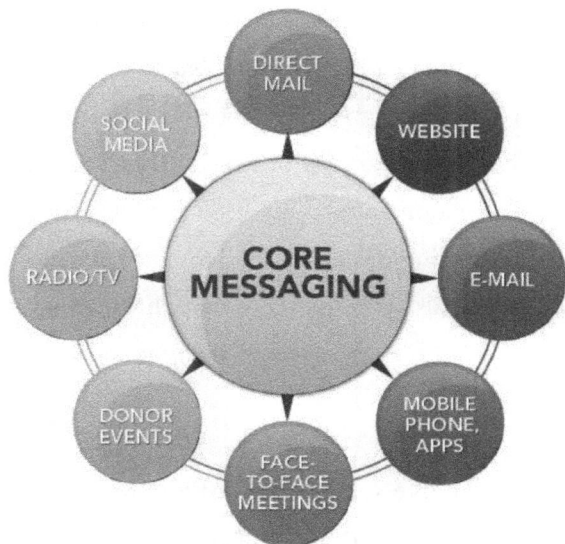

Communication Channels

A well-rounded communication strategy should model the following qualities:

STRATEGY: *Each channel should be thoughtful and planned.*
CONSISTENCY: *Each channel should convey a common message or theme.*
CONGRUENCY: *Each channel should leverage its respective strengths.*
INTENTIONALITY: *Each channel should drive toward a set of stated goals.*
INTEGRATION: *Each channel should anticipate the presence of other channels and drive the core messages of the organization*

lack continuity with our direct-mail pieces? Who is making sure that the appropriate channel is being activated for the appropriate donor at the appropriate time?

Models and diagrams such as these are invaluable for thinking comprehensively about the donor development process. But models and diagrams alone are not enough. Educational resources, such as Penelope Burk's book *Donor*

Centered Fundraising (2003) or Adrian Sargeant and Jen Shang's manifesto, *Fundraising Principles and Practice* (2010), should be required reading for anyone responsible for developing a comprehensive fundraising philosophy that will guide the strategic fund development process, especially when leaders are new to the fundraising discipline. G. Douglass Alexander and Kristina J. Carlson also provide some thought-provoking points in their book, *Essential Principles for Fundraising Success* (2005).

Strategy

Opportunities quickly surface for enhancing a fundraising program during the strategic planning process when an organization is armed with solid data and a comprehensive understanding of their philosophy of fundraising. Because the fundraising strategy is no longer limited to a few existing creative capabilities or constrained by historical tactics, the organization is free to identify development opportunities and practices that address holes in the communication and development process while promising the greatest return on the fundraising investment dollar. In keeping with my CPA friend's comment, well-versed professionals and consultants see the face looking up at them as they study organizational and donor data and strategize appropriate next steps.

In our experience, fundraising strategy is best documented in the form of a calendar—a communication and messaging plan that drives forethought and structure.

Strategic Fundraising Calendar

CHANNEL	JAN	FEB	MAR	APR	MAY	JUN	JUL	AUG	SEP	OCT	NOV	DEC
KEY MESSAGE												
DIRECT MAIL EMPHASIS												
EMAIL EMPHASIS												
EVENTS												
SPECIAL OFFERS												
WELCOME OFFERS												
WEBSITE												

Such a plan helps everyone involved in the creative execution process have valuable context for what is being communicated in any given month and how that message will be conveyed. Unexpected events and opportunities can always override the plan, but at least strategic thought was committed up front to planning for communication excellence.

A 2008 study of affluent households from the Center on Philanthropy reports that the number one reason people stopped supporting organizations is that they "no longer felt personally connected." Interestingly, the number three reason cited for ending support was "too frequent solicitations."[3] Both reasons reflect a lack of compelling communication and are often the result of not developing and executing a communication strategy based on a comprehensive foundation of data analytics and fundraising philosophy.

They are also the result of not inviting the right

---

3   Adrian Sargeant, Jen Shang, and Associates, *Fundraising Principles and Practice* (San Francisco: Jossey-Bass, 2010), 355–56.

participants to the table when the strategy was developed. Calendars like this cannot be created over a lunch with marketing to "see what we can come up with." They demand input from people who collectively bring an understanding that crosses all levels of the donor pyramid and others who intimately understand the purpose and positioning of every channel of communication. The plan should be developed annually, and then reviewed and updated quarterly.

Creative

The creative execution process (the development of copy, design, videography, event planning, web and e-mail development, and so on) and the distribution of printed and digital materials are clearly enhanced by this strategic process. When creative capabilities, not data and philosophy, drive strategy, designers and creative developers are often asked to "just create the best _____ you can."

Instead of being faced with the onerous challenge of reinventing the creative wheel every month, effective strategy provides important guidance as to what constitutes a good creative result. What are we trying to accomplish? What does the donor value? What has been said or will be said? What is relevant? What ensures this communication effort will be strategic, consistent, congruent, intentional, and integrated?

I have yet to meet an outstanding creative person—a designer, copywriter, videographer, or software developer—

who wasn't thrilled to be given direction before embarking on a creative effort. No one likes to start with a blank canvas. We all need purpose, context, and definition for how we will score a successful outcome.

Consistent execution of a fundraising strategy is certainly not a given. Books have been written on the principles of organizational execution, a subject well beyond the scope of this document. But in our experience, organizations that do a methodical job of analyzing data, documenting their philosophy of fundraising, and developing sound fundraising strategies usually have the structure important for consistent execution.

No one likes to start with a blank canvas. We all need purpose, context, and definition for how we will score a successful outcome.

One complication, however, is worth mentioning in a discussion of creative execution. While a strategic calendar may be planned in advance, the timetables for executing print, digital, and event-based programs are extremely different. While printed piece and event development timelines are measured in weeks and months, digital assets, including websites, social media posts, blogs, mobile communications, and e-mails are developed and delivered in hours and days.

Managing these two very different timetables is complicated. The answer is not to marginalize the potential of one or both mediums of communication by driving the disparate timetables toward each other. Neither will achieve maximum effectiveness if you do. Respect and cooperation must be given for the unique nature and purpose of each form, and strategies should coordinate the best way to leverage their respective strengths. Execution timelines must be coordinated—developed together, but managed independently.

Results

One of the most important decisions a nonprofit organization makes is the donor management system they use to record donor activity and report results. Many software options exist for documenting transactions and doing basic reporting. Some systems even provide the analysis needed to evaluate the results of campaigns and donor development efforts. But very few, if any, offer the kind of analytics professionals need when it comes time to start the strategic planning model all over again.

In fact, the analytics hole is so pervasive that we created our own Smart Data repository. This "warehouse" supports a suite of complex reports and analysis we use to evaluate our clients' donor relationships as reflected through giving activity and changes in activity over time. For example, our Donor Migration Report evaluates relationships across seven distinct tiers.

Once reports are run, observations are made about how donors are responding to the organization's communication efforts. New strategies can then be developed—tier by tier, channel by channel—for attracting new relationships, encouraging constituents to join the organization in its cause, and building greater levels of support for it as donor relationships mature.

Too many organizations are managing their fundraising efforts in silos. Others may not be operating in silos, but they aren't taking a data- and philosophically driven approach to developing strategy either. They use the same tactics year after year because it worked last time, and hopefully it will work again. Declines in giving revenue are balanced on the expense side of the ledger, allowing the decaying revenue cycle to continue uninterrupted.

Organizational leaders need to unlink strategy from its historical roots, where traditional tactics and creative capabilities have informed, if not driven, our fundraising strategies. We need to take the time to sift through and evaluate the volume of information at our fingertips and see what it is encouraging us to do differently.

We need to challenge each other to look for professionals with the education and experience—a well-rounded philosophy—important to connecting with donors of all types, regardless of where they fall in the pyramid or what mediums of communication they use.

What we need is to redefine fundraising in ways that will lead to incredible successes. We need a new approach to developing comprehensive donor relationship development strategies—one that begins with data that is filtered and understood through a comprehensive understanding of fundraising, relationship development, psychology and sociology, nonprofit research, and organizational understanding.

Those strategies need to be followed by consistent and outstanding creative execution, and then tracked so that results can be reevaluated during the next round of planning. Then, and only then, do we have the chance to craft fundraising strategies worthy of the nonprofit organizations we represent.

Nonprofit leaders have incredible vision—vision that can change the world. What they need is the support of fundraising professionals and programs that are prepared to make sure those visionary ideas are funded.

In the next chapter we will look at a time-tested strategy that will help you and your organization ensure that very thing.

8

The Strategic Agenda

CURT SWINDOLL

Mission statements. Core values. Vision statements. SWOT analysis. Strategic plans. While these terms, and others, have been the subject of many books and endless internal debates, confusion and frustration still reign. How do these strategic puzzle pieces fit together? And most important, how do they ultimately lead to better decisions and quantifiable impact?

Many senior nonprofit leaders fail to fully capitalize on the significant effort they've invested in defining foundational elements because (1) they don't understand each strategic component, and (2) they lack a mental picture that depicts how the various pieces connect. But make no mistake: *long-term fundraising results can only be fully realized when functional plans are driven from a sound and synergistic foundation.*

Generally speaking, frustration tends to cause leaders to do one of two things. Some choose to attend to pressing functional matters by working around strategic issues. Others invest their time defining and refining foundational elements, yet fail to integrate them into the organization's day-in, day-out execution strategies. Scott Adams of *Dilbert* fame has made a mint by mocking these mind-numbing strategic planning exercises because they rarely produce anything of substantial value!

The Strategic Agenda

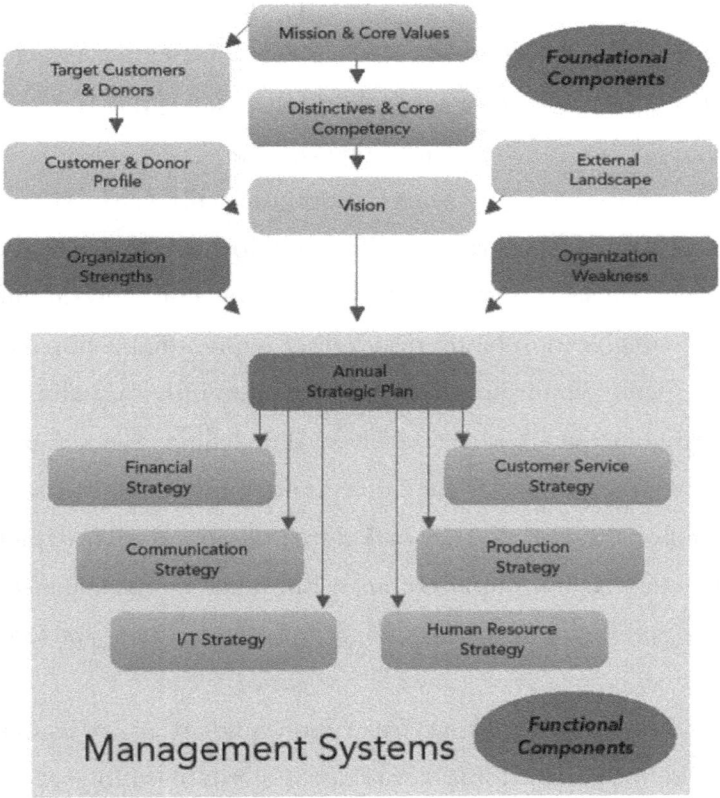

Failure to follow through on such organizational spadework eventually affects staff focus and commitment, even as it creates a host of other organizational ills. Staff members become frustrated, customers disappear, donors feel confused, and financial problems mount.

Make no mistake: long-term fundraising results can only be fully realized when functional plans are driven from a sound and synergistic foundation.

In response, let's consider a framework that links foundational elements to each other and to functional plans. Called the "Strategic Agenda Model" (see diagram), it assists leaders in understanding the strategic foundational elements in an organization, how they work together, and how they flow into a comprehensive functional plan.

This chapter offers a starting point for understanding the Strategic Agenda by presenting a *brief* definition of each element in the Strategic Agenda Model. Review each one to make sure your understanding is aligned with how the terms are used in this model. The pieces will then be assembled into a construct that reflects flow of thought and development.

Foundational Elements

Mission Statement: A broad definition of the purpose or reason an organization exists. It should address societal needs and problems, not specific products or services to be offered. Ideally, a mission statement reveals who the organization is serving, the broad problem or need it is addressing, and the societal contribution it desires to make. It rarely, if ever, changes, because the mission of the organization is substantial and ongoing.

Core Values: The values a staff emphasizes in its work with customers and donors and with each other. These values (along with the mission statement) are what make the organization unique. They are part of its core identity, essentially representing the "sign on the building." Core values are never compromised, even in times of great difficulty. (A great way to identify your organization's values is to ask, *What values do we turn to when making difficult decisions?*) They should be limited to five or six to keep them memorable and special. This may seem obvious, but core values are *values*, not products, services, goals, or outcomes. They reflect how the organization goes about its work: honor, simplicity, integrity, character, love, care, intelligence, consistency, courage, and so forth.

Target Customers and Donors: For the sake of this discussion, "customers" are the people served by an organization, while "donors" are those who offer financial and volunteer support. Customers are people an organization intends to help, as identified by the mission statement. Donors are those who are attracted to the organization's mission and how it has chosen to solve the identified societal problem or need, thereby encouraging their engagement and their financial and personal support. It is critical that an organization have some means of cost-effectively reaching its targeted customers and meeting their needs. It must also have a way of connecting with a growing base of prospective donors.

Customer and Donor Profiles: The characteristics of the customers and donors being targeted. Organizations need to not only understand their customers' needs and interests intimately, but also have some ability to meet those needs effectively and/or efficiently. Similarly, nonprofits must understand the nature of the donors who support them. Where are they? How can they be reached? What appeals to them? What do they care about and why?

Key Distinctives/Core Competencies: The unique, deeply rooted skills and abilities possessed within an organization, which it will use to create distinctive products/ services. A service is not a core competency. Growing organizations find ways to leverage one or two core competencies into a broad set of valuable products, services, and/or programs. Core competencies are not created overnight. They typically require extensive effort to develop— effort that results in tremendous expertise that is valued by society and an organization's donors and customers. An organization's brand and value proposition are often deeply rooted in the unique qualities embedded in its core competencies.

SWOT Analysis

A classic SWOT analysis is an evaluation of various elements impacting an organization's ability to thrive. They represent the Strengths, Weaknesses, Opportunities, and Threats that could alter, positively or negatively, customer interest in or donor support for what the organization is doing now or could do in the future.

Strengths and weaknesses are internal to the organization. Examples include the presence or absence of critical capabilities, valuable systems, experience, an area of expertise, a financial position, and so forth. They usually represent areas the institution has the ability to directly control or impact.

Opportunities and threats are external to the organization. They affect the nonprofit from the outside and usually represent areas the organization has little ability to directly influence. These could include the presence of competitors, the economy, the political climate, regulatory changes, demographic changes, and so forth.

Both are critical to understanding the environment in which the nonprofit is operating and the areas it may need to address in its strategic plan. Strengths should be leveraged, weaknesses eliminated, opportunities evaluated for growth potential, and threats addressed to minimize potential disruption or failure.

External Landscape: A comprehensive identification of the opportunities and threats that could potentially affect the organization. This includes alternative ("competitive") products or services—both direct and indirect—that your targeted customers might choose in place of your own offers. External landscape also addresses environmental issues, such as the economy, regulatory issues/concerns, technological developments, and anything else going on outside the organization's four walls that could influence interest in or use of the nonprofit's offerings. (See the above on SWOT Analysis.)

Vision: A clear, concise, and compelling statement (not a document!) written in measurable, dated terms that captures the organization's strategic focus for the next three or more years. No element is more important for raising funds, motivating staff, and driving the strategic focus of an institution. It is the key tool for any organization that desires to accomplish something significant. Much has been written about vision, yet leadership teams continue to adopt bland, generic phrases such as "being the best . . ." or "becoming the number one . . ." Leadership needs to decide what will be different

> *No element is more important for raising funds, motivating staff, and driving the strategic focus of an institution [than its vision]. It is the key tool for any organization that desires to accomplish something significant.*

X years from now and go after it. If one's mission describes what will be the same about an organization, then a vision states what will be different—what inspirational goal will be accomplished that will ultimately define success.[1]

Organizational Strengths/Weaknesses: Any special internal capabilities, capacities, and constraints worth noting.

---

1   For much more on vision, see chapter 6, and Pursuant's "I Have a Dream" webinar on this subject, at http://www.pursuant. com/fundraising-resources/dream-importance-vision-donor-level/.

(Again, see the SWOT Analysis for more on this.) What unique abilities do we have? What systems or processes could be of value in achieving our vision? What needs to be strengthened?

Annual Strategic Plan: A comprehensive document describing the nonprofit's funding, program/service goals, and administrative/operational plans. Details are developed for at least the next fiscal year.

More than anything, an annual plan helps ensure across-the-board alignment to the organization's vision and direction.

Key initiatives or strategies, revenue and expense projections, and operational plans should all be defined, giving leadership and staff clear direction regarding areas of extra effort and attention that will be required to achieve the vision. The plan should define each functional department's expected contribution to the vision. More than anything, an annual plan helps ensure across-the-board alignment to the organization's vision and direction.

Functional Elements

Funding Strategy: The funding and financial plans of the organization. These include a wide range of financial requirements:

- Comprehensive fundraising strategies impacting all donor giving levels and sources of support

- Reports and financial metrics critical to monitoring financial results in both revenue and expenses against plan
- Investment strategies and cash flow management

Mar-Comm Strategy: The organization's plan to present a consistent and compelling message to its customers and donors. The importance of maintaining continuity in the style and content of the "conversation" cannot be overstated. Pursuant routinely assists its clients in establishing communication themes and comprehensive plans to which all significant fundraising and stewardship messages are then connected. It is also important to address how the organization intends to create awareness of the institution's work, and how it will educate and engage donors from their first moment of contact.

Information Strategy: Much more than technology, information strategies should be driven by the information needs of the organization. They should define how the organization will generate quality, valuable data and make it available on a timely basis across departmental and application "boundaries" to anyone who needs it to make an informed decision. How will the organization effectively analyze its volumes of donor and customer data? The importance of information can be seen in the marked increase in "big data" articles being published on subjects like "donor intelligence."

Pursuant is responding to this need by making a significant investment in our own SmartData system to ensure that our clients have the information they need to drive intelligent fundraising strategies. Information strategies should also address application and reporting needs, hardware and software requirements, and security and confidentiality standards.

Program Strategy: How does your organization intend to address the continued evolution of your programs, products, and/or services? How are your programs remaining relevant to the needs of your customers? An organization's program strategy addresses the development of new products and services, as well as existing ones, ensuring the ongoing, consistent, and effective delivery of services to customers.

People Strategy: HR systems are vital in creating an effective culture that drives performance. This includes developing staff and leadership talent, creating succession plans, evaluating performance, and providing reward systems that support the kinds of behaviors the organization wants to see repeated over and over. Recruiting, onboarding, training, deploying, and retaining staff are all important elements to a complete people strategy.

Service Strategy: This strategy sets the service standards that meet and exceed customer expectations. Are customers and donors promoting the work of your nonprofit? Do they recommend your organization to their family and friends? Are they spreading the word about what you are doing? Is the staff meeting their performance standards? Are you even aware of what your donors and customers value most? Great brands may be defined in marketing, but they are built and reinforced every day through the experiences of customers and donors.

Management Systems: Surrounding all functional strategies and plans are the management and administrative tools critical to ensuring follow-through and, when necessary, making mid-course corrections. This includes identifying key metrics, holding people accountable for results, and providing liberal communication to all constituents: board, staff, volunteers, and donors.

Putting the Pieces Together

The connection of elements in the Strategic Agenda framework is simple: Higher elements must be defined before lower elements can be appropriately addressed. For example, the mission statement and core values are the absolute starting point for defining any organization. (The required degree of definition depends on several factors, including the size and complexity of the organization, the nature of the organization's products and services, the demand for what they have to offer, and so on.) But every organization should start with the mission and core values.

Vision is most effectively established when it is developed with three areas clearly defined:

- the needs/interests of the institution's target customers and donors

- a full understanding of the external environment
- the unique skills and abilities that make the organization distinctive

Vision, along with an organization's strengths and weaknesses, represents inputs to the annual strategic plan, which includes initiatives important to the foundational elements in the Strategic Agenda.

Another way to view the annual strategic plan is to see it as a road map that defines how the organization will change from its current state or condition to its desired state. The Strategic Change Model diagram to the right was originally presented in Pursuant's *The Eight Keys to Execution* white paper (see http://www.pursuant.com/fundraising -resources/whitepaper/the-eight-keys-to-execution/).

One of the most common mistakes nonprofits make is in focusing on operational needs outside the context of the strategic initiatives and vision that make their operational needs so important. We inherently know why a new building or a new donor management system or additional staff members are needed. But we often fail to define the link between those operational imperatives and their strategic counterparts.

Why is that? Because operational elements tend to be much more tangible than strategic ones. It's easier to see and touch them. Nonetheless, operational needs can be best understood only when they are linked to strategies and vision.

Strategic Change Model

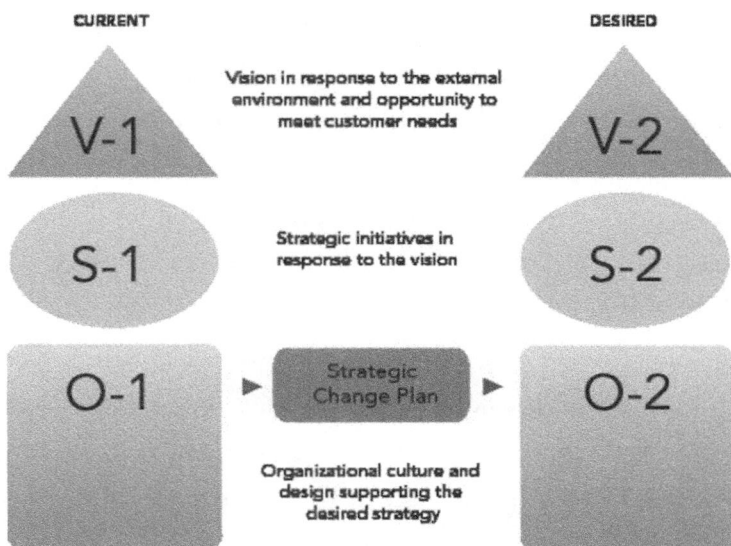

CURRENT

DESIRED

V-1

Vision in response to the external
environment and opportunity to
meet customer needs

V-2

S-1

Strategic initiatives in
response to the vision

S-2

O-1

▶ Strategic
Change Plan ▶

O-2

Organizational culture and
design supporting the
desired strategy

This is why Pursuant places so much emphasis on our clients' case statements, especially when implementing a capital campaign, a mid-level giving strategy, or an annual/ general fund program. Operational (tactical) needs must be strategically contextualized if they are to have any sense of importance in the eyes of donors.

Conclusion

Front line (functional) confusion exists because senior staff members lack a coordinated strategic direction—often because a compelling vision has not been articulated. And vision is ill defined because no one has developed a profile of target customers and donors, and leadership isn't sure what exists outside the organization's four walls.

Consider this interesting aspect in the strategic agenda framework: Managers traditionally turn to functional strategies when attempting to improve operational results or address operational pain. While changes in functional plans may be necessary, the root causes of pain or a lack of progress in an organization usually exist in foundational areas. Therefore, foundational elements must be addressed before functional plans (and staff!) can operate at peak performance.

This is why front-line tactical decisions are best made when the foundational issues are defined, understood, and aligned with other strategic elements. While every organization is (or should be!) unique in some substantial, fundamental ways, the structure of the foundational and functional components described in the strategic agenda is common to every organization.

Addressing the strategic agenda framework is the central responsibility of every nonprofit leader. Your organization has internal and external "stakeholders" who are longing to hear a consistent and compelling organizational story. These same stakeholders become staunch supporters when they observe a fully coordinated strategic message that's integrated from top to bottom.

Spend some time with your leadership team digesting and implementing your strategic agenda. The results will be better decisions, a healthier organization, more consistent fundraising results, and prolonged organizational impact.

To assist organizations in the development of their strategic agendas, Pursuant has developed two comprehensive assessments:

- An organization assessment that evaluates the strategy, design, and culture unique to nonprofit organizations. This assessment is based on documented best practices critical to organization performance.
- A fundraising assessment instrument that evaluates the strategic and execution practices of nonprofits specific to their comprehensive fundraising efforts.

Let us know if we can help your organization construct a strategic agenda that will ensure success to your fundraising efforts in the months and years ahead.

In the next chapter, we will look at the all-important topic of *accountability*. Read on.

9

Gift Officer Accountability: Where to Start

TONY SMERCINA

The mention of accountability systems for fundraisers often leads to animated discussions. Operating nonprofits with a business-oriented mind-set is nothing new. However, balancing the art and science of major gift fundraising is challenging for even the best fundraising teams. Efforts to set aside possible conflict and anxiety over accountability metrics can lead to a more empowered environment that is good for gift officers, management, and donors.

Peter Drucker said, "What's measured improves." Although it seems as if the notion of metrics is taken to extremes these days, most within the nonprofit arena would agree that improving our fundraising results begins with measurable goals and activity steps. Here, we offer some useful tips toward developing a more accountable and successful fundraising team.

In the world of annual giving, fundraising metrics are standard fare. However, some major gift operations don't embrace the same disciplines as those found in annual giving—even though the stakes are often higher. For example, just a 10 percent decline in the number of major gift donors can result in a 30 percent (or more) decline in fundraising revenue. Who can afford to leave the results to chance when there's a potential revenue swing of that magnitude on the table? It's easier for senior management and volunteers to sleep at night when clear metrics exist that are directly tied to the financial goals of the organization.

Often, gift officer management systems focus on just a few key metrics, such as number of donor visits, number of proposals, and contribution revenue. The more robust systems, *with higher probabilities of success*, measure *several* interim steps, including the number of "discovery" visits, the number of prospect "moves," the number of stewardship contacts, and so forth. But before we can dive deep into determining the various measurable steps in the process, major gift prospects must be identified, individual donor cultivation status must be determined, prospects must be assigned to gift officers, and realistic goals must be set. This chapter will explore all of these issues and position you to implement a strong accountability system.

Can We Just Hire Someone to "Do" the Major Gift Fundraising for Us?

Some view the key to success to be in the hands of HR, who sometimes receives a charge like this: "Go find a superstar development director who can get this done for us!"

Instead, CEOs and nonprofit boards must focus on building a lasting infrastructure that can adapt to changing personnel. Hiring people with the potential to be top performers is important, but they must also be surrounded by several critical program components—solid donor analytics, a powerful case message, appropriate donor stewardship, and engaged senior managers and volunteers.

Even the best major gift officers (MGOs) aren't going to stay around forever. You must guard your organization against short-term success that is highly dependent on a few key personalities. Instead, build a "culture of philanthropy" (see chapter 1) that can easily conform to changing personnel. The process by which you identify prospects, make donor assignments, set goals, execute your plan, and measure your results will become a lasting infrastructure that lives beyond the current staff and boards!

What Exactly Is a Major Gift?

The answer to this question depends on where in the fundraising life cycle the institution or organization finds itself. For some with new programs, it may be $5,000 or

$10,000. For many others, it may be $25,000, $50,000, or even more. For the purposes of this discussion, we will define a major gift as $25,000 or more. Donations of lesser amounts, even if they fit your current definition of a major gift, usually can be attracted through straightforward, short-term methods, like events, high-end direct response, and Pursuant's Charitable Partners Mid-Level Program. Securing major gifts usually requires multiple cultivation steps, and thus demands a system that measures those multiple steps toward earning a major gift.

The process by which you identify prospects, make donor assignments, set goals, execute your plan, and measure your results will become a lasting infrastructure that lives beyond the current staff and boards!

Who in Our Database Are Major Gift Prospects?

Before making portfolio assignments to your gift officers, a major gift donor pool must be established. Over the last few years it has become easier to identify donors within your constituency who possess the financial capacity to make a onetime gift of $25,000 or higher. Wealth-screening services such as Blackbaud's Target Analytics and others provide a good place to start for such information.

What does a "typical" $25,000 donor look like?

The body of knowledge around this topic is vast, but here are a few rules of thumb. Mid-career donors with the potential to make a onetime gift of $25,000-plus will typically be income earners in the mid-six-figure range or higher. Arguably, late career donors can be evaluated more in terms of their accumulated assets. Such donors must possess income-producing assets of more than $2 million (lower if gifts are made in the form of multiyear pledges).[1] This threshold can be adjusted up or down depending on the age of the donor. Retired donors, for example, with many of life's major expenses behind them, may be willing major gift prospects with lesser overall wealth. These are VERY general rules of thumb and should be viewed as just a starting point. Donor information beyond one's financial capacity tells the real story.

Once financial capacity has been identified, donor interest or affinity must be determined. Various modeling/prioritization services should consider additional factors, such as RFM (recency, frequency and monetary) analysis of past giving, and expressions of donor affinity to your cause. At Pursuant, we assign donors with a Behavioral Interest

---

1   Investment assets, excluding residential real estate and retirement assets.

Profile (BIP) score to illustrate donor affinity. BIP scores can be developed by analyzing offline behaviors, such as event attendance and volunteer participation, as well as online behaviors, such as consumption of your online content (opens and click-throughs).

The combined evaluation of wealth data, RFM, and behavioral information can help you prioritize your list of major gift prospects. This "stack ranking" of the prospect pool provides a general road map for portfolio assignments. At Pursuant, we refer to this exercise as *donor prioritization.*

How Do We Assess the Short-Term Potential of the Prospect Pool?

At some point early on in the planning process, there must be a realistic intersection between the financial goals of the organization and the short-term philanthropic potential of your base of prospective major gift donors.

> The CFO may desire a 10 percent increase in the prior year's results, or perhaps a specific project needs to be funded at a certain dollar amount.

To determine whether you can realistically achieve these targets requires an assessment of your donor prospect pool. This normally requires input from several members of your team, both staff and volunteer, who help determine where each prospect sits in the cultivation cycle. Prospect stages are used to define the donor's current status:

- **Discovery:** Capacity and affinity have been verified but no personal visits have occurred.
- **Early Cultivation:** An initial visit has occurred, but not much else.
- **Mid-Cultivation:** Multiple interactions have occurred, and the relationship is advancing.
- **Ready to Solicit:** Above-average interest in the case for support has been verified; a major gift ask will not damage the relationship.
- **Proposal Pending:** A major gift proposal has been presented to the donor.
- **Stewardship:** A previous major gift has been made; discussion about another major gift is premature.

Careful determination of the prospect stage of each donor prospect is a key step in the assessment of the short-term philanthropic potential of the overall prospect pool.

How Many Prospects Can a Gift Officer Reasonably Handle?

Establishing a portfolio size for each gift officer is a good next step. The current trend is toward smaller portfolios of 80 to 150 prospective donors. "Dunbar's Number definitely applies in this case," says Gary Cole, executive vice president of consulting at Pursuant. "Maintaining more than 150 social relationships is challenging for even the best of us. Our goal is to maximize the number of prospects who will seriously entertain a major gift proposal. It is best for each gift officer to maintain a fairly tight portfolio from the beginning." This is true even if the number of qualified prospects is significant. Prospects can always be removed (and replaced) from portfolios, so it is important to resist the temptation to create overly large portfolios.

Obviously, the total cumulative number of prospects assigned to gift officer portfolios is a function of the number of gift officers and the size of the portfolios.

How Should We Assign Prospects to Gift Officers?

The portfolio mix may differ from one gift officer to another based on circumstances such as existing relationships or the geographic locations of the gift officers. Strive for a balance between Discovery prospects (30 percent), Early and Mid-Cultivation prospects (40 percent), and Ready to Solicit/Proposal Pending prospects (30 percent). Stewardship prospects are often considered "below the line," meaning that prospects at the Stewardship stage are included in the portfolio but do not count toward the portfolio size limit.

On the first cut, gift officers who have been around for some time may end up with a disproportionate number of Stewardship prospects. Maintaining too many of these relationships can have a detrimental impact on the gift officer's ability to perform discovery, cultivation, and solicitation. Therefore, it is best to keep the number of Stewardship prospects to a minimum (fewer than the number of Discovery prospects).

Some organizations have the luxury of a stewardship department to help mitigate this potential conflict. Other, more mature programs sometimes have targeted mid-level efforts aimed at performing Discovery visits. In this case, major gift officers are only dealing with prospects who have advanced beyond the Discovery stage.

Once the portfolio assignments are complete, typically you should be ready to set your major gift fundraising goal for the year. However, you might find some unassigned prospects in the Cultivation or Ready to Solicit stages. In such cases, you may need to add gift officers or rebalance portfolios to absorb these important individuals. Adding gift officers has obvious expense implications, but the following exercise may help you determine the right time to do so. Creating the next generation of major gift donors through interaction with Discovery prospects is an important long-term strategy that cannot be ignored.

Sample Portfolio Size = 80 Sample Prospect Distribution		
# Discovery (30%) = 24	# Early & Mid Cultivation (40%) = 32	# Ready to Solicit (30%) = 24

Stewardship Prospects are typically considered "below the line" in terms of determining portfolio size.

Depending on the distribution of the overall prospect pool, not all gift officers will have a perfectly balanced portfolio. You may choose to give some younger gift officers more Discovery prospects, for example. From here, the building blocks for goal-setting begin falling into place.

How Do We Set Achievable Goals?

Sometimes, there can be a temptation to overly simplify the goal setting process. At a high level, the notion of setting goals can appear to be fairly straightforward:

> *"If we call on 100 people and 50 percent say yes, then we have 50 major gifts. If the average major gift is $10,000, then we can raise $500,000! Let's get started!"*

Unfortunately, it is not that easy. We must take into consideration the other issues that we have considered up to this point: Just what is a major gift? Who else in our database can make a major gift? How many proposals are currently pending? How many prospects will be ready to entertain a proposal (and make a decision) within the current fiscal year?

We must also evaluate how many gift officers we currently employ and then determine whether we have the human resources allocated to pursue the major gift potential that exists.[2]

You do not need sophisticated software or financial models to determine your goals. Setting the goal requires some fairly easy math that takes into consideration two key components:

> *Weighted Value of Open Proposals*
>
> +
>
> *Projected Revenue from "New Proposals"*
>
> ———————————————
>
> *2016 FUNDRAISING GOAL*

For the purposes of this exercise, let's assume we are setting goals for 2016 during the final few months of 2015 and for an organization with a December 31 fiscal year-end.

Start by evaluating the open (pending) proposals, or what some call the "proposal pipeline." Each proposal should

---

2   For the purposes of this chapter, a staff-driven fundraising model is considered. Volunteers help open doors and influence donor decision making. Volunteer-based fundraising models involve a similar process. The key difference is who is responsible for cultivating donor relationships—staff, volunteers, or both.

have an associated *probability* (odds that it will materialize at the proposed amount) and *projected close date*.

Proposal Pipeline

Prospect	Location	Proposal Amt	Proposal Date	Proj Close Date	Probabi	Weighted Value
Windsor, Dave	Nashville	$ 50,000	1/30/2015	11/1/2015	50%	$ 25,000
Cass, Joe	DC	$ 30,000	4/5/2015	11/30/2015	75%	$ 22,500
Decker, Robert	DC	$ 10,000	4/5/2015	12/1/2015	50%	$ 5,000
Rodriguez, Rich	DC	$ 10,000	5/8/2014	12/31/2015	50%	$ 5,000
Foster, Larry	Los Angeles	$ 100,000	8/1/2015	12/15/2015	75%	$ 75,000
Leonard, Jeff	Charlotte	$ 25,000	9/5/2015	12/15/2015	75%	$ 18,750
2015 Proposal Pipeline		**$ 225,000**				**$ 151,250**
Rogers, Joan	Chicago	$ 50,000	9/1/2015	1/15/2016	75%	$ 37,500
Edwards, Ron	Chicago	$ 25,000	10/1/2015	1/15/2016	25%	$ 6,250
Donatello, Bill	Philadelphia	$ 100,000	8/6/2014	2/1/2016	50%	$ 50,000
Rizzo, Bob	Chicago	$ 75,000	9/22/2015	2/15/2016	50%	$ 37,500
Simpson, Ted	Dallas	$ 25,000	8/22/2015	3/1/2016	75%	$ 18,750
2016 Proposal Pipeline		**$ 275,000**				**$ 150,000**
TOTAL PROPOSAL PIPELINE		**$ 500,000**				**$ 301,250**

First, consider the open proposals (weighted value[3]) with projected close dates after January 1 (2016 Proposal Pipeline). Next, assume that some proposals in the 2015 pipeline will roll over into 2016. A rule of thumb would be to carry forward into 2016 one-third of the weighted value of the 2015 open proposals. As you get closer to the end of the fiscal year, you can continually adjust the "rollover" proposal amount.

> *2016 Open Proposals (weighted value) = $150,000*
> +
> *2015 "Rollover" Proposals (33% X $151,250) = $49,912*
> +
> *Projected Revenue from "New Proposals"*
>
> *2016 FUNDRAISING GOAL*

---

3   Weighted Proposal Value = Proposal Value X Probability to Close

Now, let's figure out how much of the goal will be derived from "New Proposals." We have to review the assessment of each prospect in the portfolio. In this example, let's assume the gift officer has a fairly balanced portfolio with 30 percent of the prospects in the Ready to Solicit stage. With a portfolio of 80 prospective donors, that equals 24 Ready to Solicit Prospects. Our sample organization has a historical Close Rate[4] of 50 percent and projects an average major gift of $30,000.

	2016 New Proposal Activity
# Ready to Solicit Prospects	24
Projected Close Rate	50%
Projected # Major Gifts	12
Projected Average Gift	$ 30,000
Projected Revenue from New Proposals	$ 360,000

We can now add up all of the elements of the goal for 2016. This gift officer has a projected 2014 goal of $560,000!

2016 Open Proposals (weighted value) = $150,000
+
33% of 2015 Open Proposals (33% X $151,250) = $49,912
+
Projected Revenue from "New Proposals" = $360,000
_____

2016 FUNDRAISING GOAL = $559,912

Again, the goal may ultimately increase based on proposals that roll over from 2015 to 2016. Considering this possibility provides incentive to finalize the gift in 2015.

_____

4   Percentage of proposals that become major gifts

Some organizations may have higher personal expectations for their gift officers, which may or may not be realistic. Taking this recommended approach will help ensure that achievable goals are established that properly assess the organization's short-term philanthropic potential.

What Are the Next Steps?

Finally, you have your prospects identified and assigned. Contribution revenue goals have been set. Now, you can move on to developing a measurement system to help increase the probability of achieving those goals.

But sometimes there's a problem. Before you can mount a fundraising campaign that reaches any goals at all, you've got to have the budget for it. And what if your budget has been steadily or even radically shrinking? In the next chapter we will talk about how you can *resurrect* your declining annual fund.

10

Resurrecting a
Declining Annual Fund

TRENT RICKER

During the Great Recession, nonprofit organizations faced the common challenge of making cuts in their fundraising budgets. And waning budgets usually translate to a necessary reduction in staff and the size of an organization's fundraising investment. As a result, the annual fund was one of the hardest-hit areas of many nonprofits' budgets. And the outcomes were predictable: declining revenue and lapsed donors. Why? Because the component of the overall fundraising program that supports the operating budget and is an important source for the next generation of major donors had been compromised.

It's been almost a decade since the Great Recession began, yet many organizations still face floundering annual funds. Unfortunately, the commonality of this persistent problem has led organizations to adopt a certain level of acceptance of this poor performance. After all, it's easy to justify declining revenue and a smaller donor file when you're asked to cut your investment. How could anyone expect to see an increase in revenue when the amount of the investment is being reduced and donors are dealing with the worst economy in decades?

As the economy has improved, many organizations haven't followed at an appropriate pace by ramping up to prerecession investment levels. Instead, boards have adapted to the "new reality" of these current giving levels and are now charging their fundraising leadership to increase revenue . . . without increasing the budget.

In addition, a board may be pushing to resume the capital campaign that got postponed during the recession. So they ask the organization's leaders to evaluate how the nonprofit can not only increase its annual fund, but also embark on a planning study to prepare for a campaign.

"It's not fair!" one such leader states. Perhaps. But it is reality.

Such is the life of fundraising leadership post–Great Recession. So how do you cope? What can you do to resurrect your annual fund that has seen declines since 2008 and has had trouble turning the corner to trend back toward prerecession levels?

A wise man once told me, "Anyone can do more with more. Good leaders can do more with the same. But it takes exceptional leaders to do more with less." During this new reality, exceptional fundraising leaders need to figure out how to "do more with less." And the task may not be as daunting as it sounds.

Don't Get Too Tempted by Traditional Acquisition

A frequent tactic I hear blurted out to resurrect a declining annual fund is, "We need to reinvest in acquisition. Look at the chart! When we stopped investing in acquisition back in 2009, everything went down! Let's do a big acquisition campaign, and things will get back on track!"

There's no argument that acquisition is a key component to a healthy annual fund. And most organizations did, in fact, cut acquisition over the past few years, which naturally contributed to the decline in their donor files.

However, this decline is not simply due to attracting fewer new donors. Churn in your file is defined as new donors minus lapsed donors. If that number is positive, you're growing. If it's negative, you're shrinking. Pretty simple.

"Anyone can do more with more. Good leaders can do more with the same. But it takes exceptional leaders to do more with less." During this new economic reality, exceptional fundraising leaders need to figure out how to "do more with less." And the task may not be as daunting as it sounds.

Remember, you aren't the only nonprofit that suffered a declining fundraising program during the recession. Therefore, you aren't the only one who's considering jumping back into the acquisition game. As many organizations dive back into the mail acquisition pool, you can only imagine the deluge of requests for support that are being poured out on our population. Competition is fierce for new dollars. So how would you make your message stand out?

Acquisition is very important, but our tactics need to be evaluated. Consider innovative strategies such as organic online name acquisition, peer-to-peer acquisition, or new innovative events. Additionally, you should plan to follow up your acquisition programs with an intentional conversion process that quickly moves new donors to mid-level donors.[1] New donor retention is all about converting that first gift into another and then another. This is a key strategy that should be focused on within the first ninety days after a donor gives his first gift. Get him in a relationship pathway, and then thank him, tell him how his gift made a difference, share more about your nonprofit and why it's important, and then

---

1   My colleague Curt Swindoll recently wrote an important piece on this subject titled "Redefining Acquisition," which can be found at www.pursuant.com/fundraising-resources/redefining -acquisition/. It includes an acquisition calculator (www.pursuant .com/redefining-acquisition/calculator/) that makes a strong case for the true potential of an intentional conversion process following acquisition.

ask for his additional support. Ask him to give another gift, participate in an event, volunteer, or even advocate for your organization. You need to get your donors more involved and build their loyalty.

Reactivation: The Key to Resurrection

While we should focus on both sides in the "new donors minus lapsed donors" equation, the more important one is the number of lapsed donors. These folks have supported your organization in the past. We've all heard the commercial truism that it's easier to sell more to an existing customer than it is to acquire a new one. That holds true in fundraising as well.

Reactivation is an often-overlooked strategy that focuses on those donors who gave at one time but have stopped giving. Generally, these people fall into two categories: those who gave only once, and those who gave more than once.

Every day that goes by that you aren't talking to your lapsed donors, you can be sure that someone else is. The cardinal sin of fundraisers is to accept

Every day that goes by that you aren't talking to your lapsed donors, you can be sure that someone else is.

lapsed donors as being just a part of life and then rushing to replace them through acquisition. This doesn't need to be a matter of acquisition OR retention. It's actually a solution of intentional acquisition AND retention. However, sometimes the importance of reactivation gets lost in that equation. So many donors were lost over the past several years that reactivation must be a core tactic of your resurrection plan.

Of course, this should lead you to ask some broader questions: What is our general retention strategy? What are we doing when a donor lapses, whether it's a first-time donor or a renewing donor (one who gave a second gift but hasn't given anything since then)? Do we implement a pre-lapse strategy to curtail donor drop-off when certain behaviors indicate that a donor may not give again? What is our re-activation strategy for those donors who haven't renewed?

Key Multi-year Donors: Your Lifeblood

Donors who gave gifts over consecutive years are the golden goose of the annual fund. These supporters proved they weren't just one-hit wonders who gave episodically in response to a great appeal or an environmental event. They gave once. And then they gave again the next year. And again the next year.

So why did some of these donors lapse? Research tells us people stop giving for a variety of reasons: they don't feel appreciated; they weren't asked again; they are giving to another organization; they feel disconnected from the organization; they feel they were being asked to give too often. Which of these factors are within your control? All of them.

Naturally, during the Great Recession people couldn't always afford to give more. But research also tells us that while people gave a smaller amount of money overall, they tended to cut back by giving to fewer organizations than they used to. For instance, an individual who used to give $100 per year to five different organizations may have continued to give to only three of those groups during the recession. However, it's likely that this person gave more money to each one. Giving $125 to three favorite organizations equals $375 per year, which is still less than the $500 per year this person used to donate. You get the idea.

Here's what likely happened when you cut your budget. Stewardship was slashed. Acquisition was cut. You may have even shortened the definition of "current donor" from someone who gave within the past 24 months to those who gave within the past 12 or 18 months.

After making such changes, what would you expect the end result to be? Might a donor who's given to you every year over the past few years suddenly feel underappreciated? Would he feel disconnected? Might he have started giving to a different organization that wisely chose to continue to invest in acquisition and stewardship? Pretty logical stuff.

So what can we do about it now? We can talk to our lapsed donors in a very special way. We can appeal to them in a way that is genuine and transparent. We can tell them we miss them and need their support now more than ever.

If you gathered a group of your supporters who used to give you $100 per year from 2005 through 2008 but then stopped giving in 2009 and beyond, what would you say to them? Might you ask your CEO to address them? Would you show them the progress you've made since they left . . . and perhaps what could have been done if only they'd continued their support? Would you ask them to consider coming back to you?

An important strategy for resurrecting your annual fund is to focus on this key group of donors. What sort of inexpensive, yet impactful packaging would prompt them to open your letters or e-mails? What would your messaging be? Should it be a letter from your CEO or perhaps an engaging video of your staff delivering a heartfelt "We want you back . . . We need you!" message?

Reactivating lapsed donors makes financial sense. That's because reactivated donors have repeatedly shown a propensity to give and be retained at higher levels than new donors. In addition, reactivation strategies represent a "zero-risk" opportunity—oftentimes you're guaranteed to at least break even on the costs of implementing them, while many will even generate new net revenue.

Reactivating lapsed donors makes financial sense. That's because reactivated donors have repeatedly shown a propensity to give and be retained at higher levels than new donors.

Consider the scenario on the following page:

Lapsed Donors	1,000
Reactivation Percentage	10%
Reactivated Donors	100
Average Reactivated Gift	$100
Total Initial Reactivated Gifts	$10,000
Cost of Reactivation	$6,000
Net Revenue from Reactivation	$4,000
Reactivated Donor Retention	45%
Retained Reactivated Donors	45
Subsequent Gifts per Retained Donor	$200
Second Year Reactivated Donor Giving	$9,000
Total Two-Year Giving from Reactivated Donors	$13,000

Most organizations have far more than 1,000 lapsed donors who generate gifts well above the $100 level represented in this chart. For example, if your organization has 10,000 lapsed donors and experiences average gifts of $250, giving from reactivated donors from just the first two years would total more than $300,000—and that doesn't include gifts in the third and subsequent years, or the value of upgrading reactivated donors to mid or major giving levels!

Zero-Sum Game

In this new economic reality, fundraising budgets are pretty much a zero-sum game. It's very difficult to get additional budget funds unless you can create the business case to forecast the positive impact on revenue.

The limiting belief is that you need to spend more to get more. While it's probably true that you would get more if you spent more, an important angle has to be prioritizing your current budget.

You remember the definition of insanity, don't you? It's doing the same thing over and over while expecting a different result. You can't continue to do the same segmentation, the same appeals, and the same stewardship and expect your program to magically take a turn for the better just because the economy has improved.

Instead, start looking more closely at innovative acquisition strategies and prioritized segmentation. Test some name acquisition strategies online and cultivate them in a low-cost manner to convert people to that first gift. Concentrate on a next-gift strategy that will quickly cultivate new donors into additional engagement. And finally, go back to those key donors who left you . . . and humbly ask them to come back.

So there you have it. We have talked about everything from how to turn big data into donations, to successfully creating a culture of philanthropy, to developing a stewardship strategy that decreases losses and increases gains—and more. We hope that this information has helped you—as you begin to use it in your future efforts, we *know* it will. Implement the strategies we have discussed in these chapters, and you and your organization will accelerate your impact. We guarantee it.

About the Authors

Trent Ricker currently leads Pursuant as chief executive officer, casting vision for the company while also playing a key role in business development and client service. With over 20 years of senior management and consulting experience, Trent is involved in client fundraising strategy development with a pronounced emphasis on the nonprofit application of business intelligence services.

Gary M. Cole, EdD, CFRE, is executive vice president. He leads consulting teams and provides executive-level organizational management and philanthropic counsel. With nearly a quarter century of fundraising experience, Gary's main areas of expertise include major gifts strategy, planned giving, and campaign planning and management.

Allison Lewis Lodhi, CFRE, is senior vice president. She excels at identifying organizational opportunities, implementing strategic initiatives, and maximizing resources. These talents inform Allison's approach for developing integrated, cross-channel fundraising strategies that are holistic, scalable, and focused on results.

Tony Smercina, is executive vice president. He leads Pursuant's activities in higher education, collegiate sports, Greek organizations, and independent schools. He also provides gift officer services for upgrading loyal annual/general fund donors to mid-level giving and beyond.

Curt Swindoll is executive vice president. He leads Pursuant's work with faith-based organizations as well as the Direct Response practice group. His career has spanned six industry sectors, serving or consulting in operations, sales and business development, marketing and branding, IT and software development, and fundraising.

About Pursuant

Pursuant began in 2001 with a single goal: to help nonprofits raise more money. This singular focus has remained over the years as the organization has grown and our approach has been refined.

The road to this crucial discovery began in 2001, when founder Matt Frazier sought to help organizations tell more effective stories through short-form video to move constituents to action. By 2007, Pursuant was serving hundreds of clients, integrating services from the top of the donor pyramid to the bottom, and across every communication channel. Charitable Partners was acquired in 2008 to augment our annual fund solutions with a revolutionary mid-level giving model. Viscern was acquired in 2009, adding major gifts to the offering. Finally, in 2010, KMA Direct Communications was acquired for its expertise in direct response fundraising and data analysis.

Today, Pursuant exists to achieve the exact same goal as when we began: to help nonprofits raise more money than ever before. We believe that intelligent fundraising is the key driver to helping nonprofits raise more money and affect more lives. We work tirelessly to ensure that our clients see a dramatic difference in their fundraising results. We take great pride in serving our clients as they embark on missions to help make the world a better place.

Pursuant has the opportunity to work alongside nonprofit organizations in every sector, including education, collegiate athletics, faith-based organizations and ministries, health care, health and human services, arts and culture, and churches. Our services include fundraising strategy, donor acquisition and upgrade programs, analytics and business intelligence modeling, capital campaign counsel and major gift development services, mid-level giving programs, direct response fundraising services, and gift officer training services.

The Pursuant Leadership Team

Trent Ricker, Chief Executive Officer

Ross Miller, Chief Operating Officer

Curt Swindoll, Executive Vice President, Strategy

Gary Cole, Executive Vice President, Principal

Tony Smercina, Executive Vice President, Principal

Rebecca Gregory Segovia, Executive Vice President, Client Strategy

Twitter: @Pursuant

Facebook: Pursuant

LinkedIn: Pursuant

Web: www.pursuant.com

Blog: www.pursuant.com/blog